RENEW4D

Small Habits, Big Impact: Renew Your Life One Step at a Time

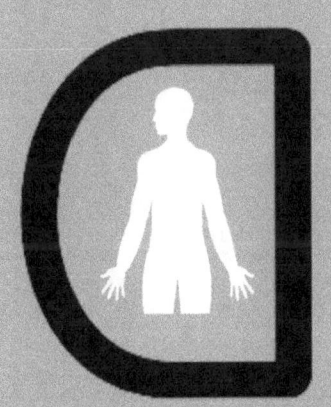

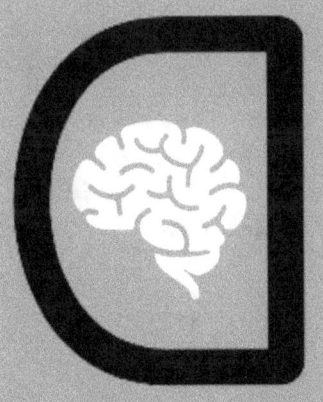

Jessee Lovaas

www.Renew4D.com
Follow me @Renew4D
Instagram / Facebook / TikTok / Youtube / X / LinkedIn

Dedication

I dedicate this book to everyone who woke up one morning and thought, 'There has to be more!' Whether you're 20 or 45, whether you're just starting or starting over, this book is for anyone ready to stop settling.

Have you ever thought, "there has to be more!"

You want to know a secret?

…there is!

CONTENTS

Acknowledgements

I would like to thank my wife, Rebekah, for putting up with me and my crazy, wild ideas. I want to thank my kids, Henry and Savannah, for teaching me how to be a parent and for showing me the difference between a leader in the marketplace and one in the home.

Thank you, Mom and Dad. Your support throughout my entire life has not been taken for granted. You've paid the way to internships, bought fancy Abercrombie clothes when we didn't have the money, and you always sowed advice, wisdom, caution, and money into my adventures. I literally wouldn't be here without you.

To my sister, who's been an inspiration to me. She's overcome so much in her life, and it's fantastic to see who she's become. And she was the first and BEST author in our family.

I would like to thank the following people who have been instrumental in my life, leadership, and formation as the person I am today. (In no particular order)

JT Adkins, Phil Buechler, Rick Bennett, Lance Weibye, James Hensley, Brian Kangas, Barry O'Neal, Craig & Linni Weishar, Rachel Pastukhov, Geri Anderson, Dani Langevin, Jeff Phillips, Steve Sims, Ricky Bennett, Carl Wesley Anderson, Jake Booher, Richard Green...who I'm still holding on to that prophetic word from 2004.

These people have zero personal relationship with me, but have also been instrumental in my life. Their books, podcasts, social media posts, insights, music, and wisdom have shaped and molded me into the person I am today. (In no particular order)

John Bevere, Craig Groeschel, Louie Giglio, Matt Redman, Dave

Ramsey, Ed Mylett, Max Lugevere, Gary Brecka, Mark Hyman, Mel Robbins, Tony Robbins, Joe Rogan, Rob Dial, John Eldridge, Brian & Jenn Johnson, Simon Sinek, Andrew Huberman, Gary V, Robin Sharma, James Clear, Russell Brunson, Justin Whitmel Earley, John Maxwell, Christine Caine, Tara-Leigh Cobble, John Mark Comer, the Helsers, the Torwalts, Jason Upton.

Introduction

A Mid-Life Crisis...

In February of 2023, I was in New York City for a work trip. Anyone who's been to New York knows that you get your steps in there. Not to mention heavy moving, setup, and teardown of a tradeshow. During this week, it became infinitely complex to walk, bend, or move. My lower back had been killing me for some time, and now the sciatic nerve has joined in to say hello. Once the nerve was hit, I literally couldn't walk. So the streets of New York were not pleasant on that trip.

For the next 6 months, it got worse. I was seeing a chiropractor multiple times a week. started going to a joint and pain doctor. I had an epidural, which was the most painful experience in my life, and it did nothing to help. Eventually, I found my way to a brain and spine neurosurgeon. Long story short, he recommended a fusion of my L4 and L5. I didn't want surgery, but I've exhausted all other remedies with no success. I agreed to the surgery.

I woke up one morning, at 40 years old, and just freaked. I totally had a mid-life crisis starting. I'm 40. My body is failing. I'm gaining weight. I'm balding and greying. I hurt. I can't play with my kids at the level I want to. I can't put them to bed or pick them up at times. And my job...was a job. Who the heck am I? What am I doing? Where am I going? Is this the best life God had in store for me?

It was rough. In the midst of all of this, we were struggling with my sons' behavior at home. After almost two years of tests and appointments, he was diagnosed on the spectrum with high-functioning autism. Between physical pain, emotional stress of parenting, being the only source of income for my family, and now an autistic son whom I can't effectively parent, I felt lost and defeated. Depressed. Depressed enough to have my doctor put me on antidepressant medication. I was just a wreck in all areas of my life.

Fast forward to September of 2023. I had a three-week stint of work trips, back-to-back, cross-country. Nashville (my home) to Seattle for a week, and back. Two days later to LA for a week, and back. 3 days later to New York City again for 9 days, and back. tons of walking. Lots of heavy moving and tradeshow setups. Did I mention lots of walking? Not to mention six flights, which didn't help my back at all. I knew I needed a change. Unfortunately, it had to start after my back surgery.

I had surgery in November of 2023. It was the first Thanksgiving I didn't cook the turkey. It was the first Christmas that my yard wasn't the brightest in the neighborhood. I was lame inside and out. But, healing. What I didn't realize then was that it wasn't just my body that was healing. It was my mind, soul, and spirit as well.

I was supposed to be bedridden for a few weeks, and not travel, or do anything strenuous, or lift anything heavy. But life happened. Two days after surgery, my wife got strep and had to be quarantined. So, days after back surgery, I was up, taking care of everyone. A month after my surgery, my mom had emergency triple-bypass surgery...the widow maker. I flew to Oregon. I had to ask very nice strangers to lift my bag above the seat and back down on my flights. It was humbling. But it was another wake-up call.

My parents were "young" at the time, in their 60s. But they had a hard life physically, with multiple bouts of cancer, bone and back issues, and a long list of ailments. most of which were "hereditary", so I thought. I was looking at my future and got scared. But the fear didn't last long. It finally stopped. I decided in my heart to do whatever it takes not to need a walker at my kid's graduation. Not to be overweight and out of breath for the daddy-daughter dance at her future wedding. I need to make some serious changes. Every aspect of my life needed help. Body, soul, mind, and spirit—the four foundational areas we'll explore in depth throughout this book.

Where did I start? In the beginning.

John 1:1 says, "In the beginning was the word, and the word was with god, and the word was god." I needed to start where the world started. In the beginning. The word. With God, which is why we'll begin our renewal journey with the spirit in Part 2.

Over the next two years, to this very moment of writing this book, I embarked on a journey to rekindle my relationship with god, change my paradigms and thought processes, add and subtract habits, cleanse my soul, and live a healthier life. I was determined to be vibrant, healthy, and cognisant enough to play with my grandchildren someday, and god willing, even see my great-grandkids. I will not be hindered, for my wife or my kids, any longer.

What you're about to read is a 4-step process to renew every area of your life. I'm not claiming to have discovered something new—this is two decades of wisdom I've gathered from mentors, books, and podcasts, consolidated into one practical guide. Think of it as the highlight reel: a little Simon Sinek, a dash of Craig Groeschel, some Ed Mylett, and a whole lot of Jesus. By the end, you'll have the tools to renew your life using the 4 D's.

Small habits make a big impact. I Renew4D my life; body, soul, mind, and spirit...one step at a time. **Will you?**

PART 1

THE 4 D's

1. WHAT ARE THEY?

At some point in life, I think anyone who has ever been to church, gone on a diet, read a book, or been in a leadership meeting at work has heard some concocted form of the following...

Information, Application, Occupation.

The 3 "fill in the blanks" of success.

Follow these 10 guidelines to achieve a Chris Hemsworth-esque physique.

5 easy steps to financial freedom.

Sow $1,000 to this Nigerian prince and you'll magically grow your hair back. NOTE...this did NOT work for me.

I am no different, though. I have a long history of experience in performance management and leadership development. I've trained CEO's, and discipled teenagers into future leaders. I've also been on the other end of the stick. I've been the one in the chair needing counseling or attending days-long meetings about "culture" or "MORS."

Throughout my tenure as a leader, both in the marketplace and in the church, I've developed my own system, a guideline of sorts. I've used it countless times when discipling and mentoring people. I've used it myself, and on others. It works. It's purpose-oriented. It's goal-centric. It's explorative and informative. It's habit-building. It's behavior shaping. It's God focused. And most importantly, it is renewing, in all areas of your life: body, soul, mind, and spirit. You'll see this theme throughout the book.

Most people don't lack motivation; they lack structure. They start with excitement but stall when life gets hard or unclear. The Four D's give you a compass when your goal feels foggy, a framework when your habit gets hard, and a guide when your calling seems out of reach.

That was my main problem. No structure. I had all the motivation i the world. A "better life" for my wife and kids, be healthier, lose weight, make more money, have a bigger house, quit my current job, work for myself, and be on my own schedule. Easy right? Yeah, not so much. I knew there was more to this life than what I was living. I had higher aspirations, bigger dreams, unmet goals, and callings unfulfilled. I needed more than the ambition and motivational "wants". I needed a system to help me get there.

I remember standing in that Christian school classroom at 5 AM, mopping floors because my salary had been cut in half. That's when God spoke clearly: 'What you've done so far has been on your own power. What I'm calling you to will require mine alone.' That moment forced me to start over completely. I had to discover who I really was, develop new habits and skills, deploy them in the real world, and eventually help others do the same. I didn't know it then, but I was walking through what I now refer to as the Four D's.

The Four D's serve as a guideframe that you can use for any area of your life, any goal, any habit, or any dream. In Parts 2-5, we'll show you exactly how to apply this framework to your spirit, mind, soul, and body. The Four D's help give your goals structure. They help you go deeper into the "Why?" of each goal. They help you think about the importance of the goal or habit, what you want out of it, and how it will benefit your future career, family, and success.

What are the Four D's? I'm glad you asked. In a nutshell...

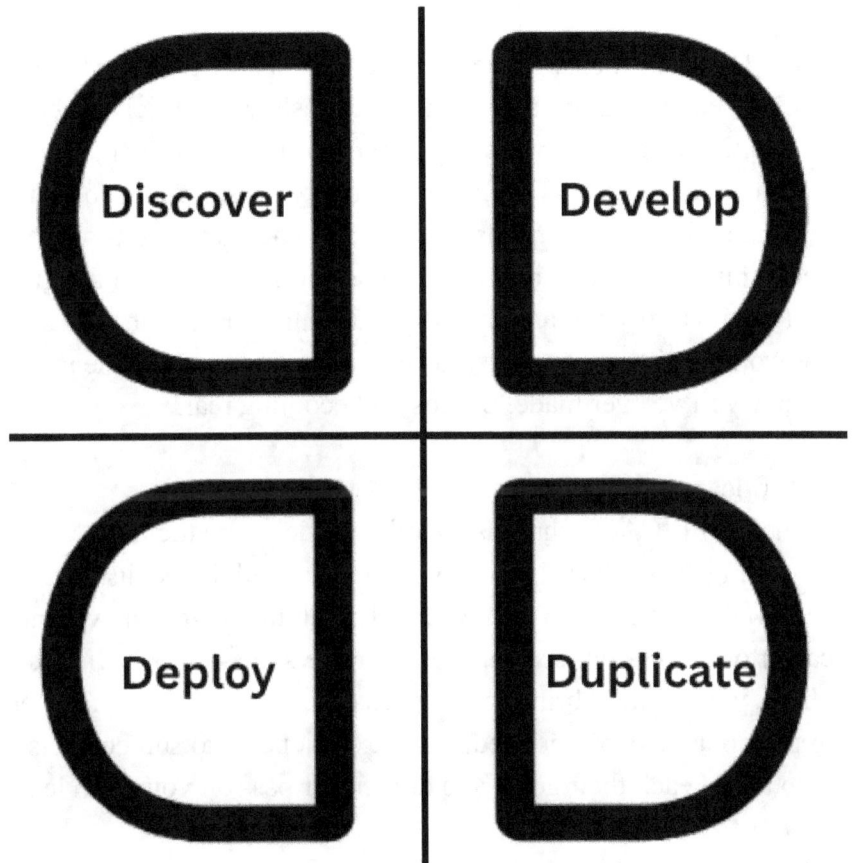

Discover:

The DISCOVER phase is informational. Little to no cost. Longest phase. This is a private phase. No one knows about this unless you bring them into your circle of trust. Google and YouTube are your best resources in this phase.

Develop:

The DEVELOP phase is the application phase. You start to incur a little cost now, as you begin to invest in books, podcasts, or supplements. This is the phase in which you begin to apply what you've learned and discovered. This is still a fairly private phase, but you're starting to step out a little, making your journey more public.

Deploy:
The DEPLOY phase is the "occupation" phase. This is where what you've been doing privately is now being shown publicly. There is an additional cost as you begin to branch out on your own, such as starting a business or adding higher-quality subscriptions to your resources. This phase means that some of your new habits are becoming routine, and many new things are becoming an integral part of your daily life and identity. This is the hardest phase. A lot of the work is still on you, but you're also starting to make the most money you've ever made. Success is becoming real.

Duplicate:
The DUPLICATE phase is what I consider to be the most rewarding. This phase is when you've mastered the habits. You've achieved some goals. You are actively walking in your newfound career or profession, or whatever your life's mission was. In this phase, you begin to bring in disciples or legacy branches. You begin to pour out years of knowledge and experience into someone else, to help them reach their goals and dreams, or pass on your own legacy.

I am a woodworker and an avid fan of This Old House. So think about it like this. The 4 D's are like building a house:

Discover is the blueprint.
Develop is the construction.
Deploy is living in it.
Duplicate is inviting others in or building another.

Before we dive deeper, ask yourself:

- What am I currently trying to build in my life?
- Which D am I currently stuck in?
- Where have I quit in the past?

Ecclesiastes 3 reminds us that there is a season for everything. **Discover** is a season of learning. **Develop** is a season of planting. **Deploy** is a season of working. **Duplicate** is a season of harvesting. God also works in seasons. And the Four D's help you walk through yours faithfully.

So where are you right now? Discovering? Developing? Deploying? Duplicating? No matter the answer, the good news is this: you're not lost, you're just in a phase. The Four D's will give your chaos a pattern, your vision a process, and your effort a return. This book is your guide. Grab a notepad, take a deep breath, and let's begin the process of renewing every dimension of your life.

2. DISCOVER

I remember it as clear as day. It was early in the morning, maybe around 5 am. I was mopping a Christian school's classroom floor as a part-time janitorial job during COVID, when my company reduced my salary by half. I used that time a lot to pray, seek God, and worship.

It was some of the most impactful moments with the Lord I've ever had...quietly cleaning toilets. It was October 7th, 2020. It was one of those "audible voice" moments from God. He spoke as clearly as you talking to someone on the phone. He said, "What you've done with your career so far has all been done on your own power and strength. What I am calling you to will require mine and mine alone."

That rocked me. I've always taken pride in how far I've come, given that I grew up with no money and no college experience. I've always worked my way up in jobs, usually into management of some sort. But now, God is telling me it's all been done on my own, which it has.

That moment catapulted me into the foundations of this book. And it started with Discovery. I had to scrap it all, start from the beginning, and rediscover who I am and what God is calling me to. I was 38 at the time, so just a few years before my back surgery and mid-life crisis.

This "late" in life, I was forced to throw everything out that I've done and accomplished, and look for the road less traveled. A harder road. One with uncertainty and quite honestly, a road that scared the living you know what out of me. I knew that day my life was about to get a lot harder and way more uncomfortable. But I needed to rediscover my identity.

The Discover phase begins with our identity. As 2 Corinthians 5:17 states, *"Therefore, if anyone is in Christ, the new creation has come: The old has gone, the new is here!"*
If we are in Christ, we have a new *identity*. Any time we decide to make a change in our lives, our identity changes. It evolves. You can transition from a poverty mindset to one of prosperity. You can go from depression and anxiety to peace and confidence. The basis of our life's mission starts with our identity. The sooner we discover this, the sooner we can begin implementing the next phases.

What better way to start than in the beginning? Literally. John 1:1 says, "In the beginning was the Word, and the Word was with God, and the Word was God." You can't expect to find your identity, or your why, until you start at the beginning...with God. You need a relationship with Jesus to be truly Renew4D and to find the strength to fight for your future.
As you begin to establish new routines and habits, hopefully creating a morning routine that includes dedicated quiet time for prayer, studying the Word, building a relationship with Jesus, and journaling, keep this in mind. Start your day with Thanksgiving! In fact, Jesus even teaches us how to do that.

<u>The Lord's Prayer</u>
Matthew 6:9-13

This, then, is how you should pray:
"'Our Father in heaven,
hallowed be your name,
your kingdom come,
your will be done,

17

on earth as it is in heaven.
Give us today our daily bread.
And forgive us our debts,
as we also have forgiven our debtors.
And lead us not into temptation,
but deliver us from the evil one.

Jesus starts his prayer with thanksgiving. He starts with the adoration of the father. Before He even asks for anything, He praises God and gives thanks. This is how we should start our days and begin our discovery journey.

In a recent episode of The Ed Mylett Show, Ed explains: "People yo-yo in life because they work on the external mechanics and not the internal identity." Don't focus so much on the temporal or what's going on, on the outside. Focus on the internal and the eternal, and what's going on, on the inside. It's a divine discontentment. Celebrate your victories, no matter how small. Don't delay happiness. Have fun with the wins, and continue to push past any losses that may happen. Will your identity be someone who pushes forward and grows into a person of consistency? Or will it be someone who gives up?

The Discover phase is the first phase of any journey or habit-building process, because it's literally *the* discovery phase. You're learning and gathering information. This phase may be about your spiritual growth, as you discover more about God and who He is in your life. You're discovering ways to increase the time spent with Him and build a stronger relationship. In business, it could involve learning how to start a business, change careers, or choose the right college to attend. Or even how to be a better parent or spouse.

Discovery is quite possibly the longest phase, simply because it never ends. You will never stop discovering more about God, yourself, business, education, or parenting. Leaders read, and good leaders learn constantly. The minute you stop learning is the minute you start to decrease and wither away.

Take a trip with me...and Bill & Ted. Socrates once said, *"An unexamined life is not worth living."* And Galileo said, *"All truths are easy to understand once they are discovered; the point is to discover them."* These two ancient philosophers knew that discovering your identity is the key to unlocking your life's divine plan.

The Discover phase, without taking notes, is a wasted phase of life. How can you learn without writing it down, rereading it, analyzing it, digesting it, and committing it to memory? You need to learn how to take good notes or keep a journal. Writing those nuggets of truth down is so important. Anything of value that you find needs to be written down. Otherwise, it will eventually go out the other ear, lost and forgotten. I highly encourage you to purchase my Renew4D Daily Journal to accompany you along this book and your new journey.

You need to become a sponge for anything and everything. You must use your gut and discernment on many things. You can't just take the internet or a podcast at its word. But to discover is to gather. Take advantage of social media.

In his podcast, Dan Martell advises curating your social media to your advantage. As you listen and learn, follow everything you can from someone who resonates with you. If I'm listening to a podcast and hear someone I've never heard of before, and I like what they are saying or it resonates with me, I immediately follow their Instagram and TikTok, as well as any other form of media or resource I can find from them. I want my feed to be filled with new insight and information from these people. I want to constantly be learning, even when I'm just scrolling.

To Discover means to find your "why". I'd like to take credit for that, but there are numerous books on the topic, more specifically, as Simon Sinek writes in "Find Your Why." Your WHY is the foundation of your future. Your WHY is why you get up every day to do the thing you feel called to do. Find your WHY, find your pathway.

More importantly, sharing your WHY with the world will push you to commit to it and back up your words with actions. The more you give voice to your intentions, the more likely you'll be to follow through with them.

In this Discover phase, you need to...
1. Find your *identity* (your why, your purpose)
2. *Prepare*
3. Change your *Paradigm*
4. Find your *People* (mentors, leaders, and friends).

Lastly, the discover phase goes hand-in-hand with the MIND section later in this book. You'll see how many of the D's directly correlate to body, soul, mind, and spirit. That's the basis of this book. However, in discovery, it's essential to shift your perspective on your identity.

"You'll never outperform the way you see yourself."

- Ed Mylett

Reread that again. This is a truth we'll dive deeper into when we explore renewing your mind in Part 4.

Your words become your future. Proverbs 23:7 says, *"For as a man thinks in his heart, so is he."* It's not "fake it until you make it", it's declare it with confidence, in your heart and mind, until you become it. You are who you say and think you are. Henry Ford famously said, "Whether you think you can, or you think you can't...you're right."

There is a difference between looking the part and feeling the part. Lots of people look wealthy or successful, but they don't feel that way in the slightest. I don't want to look rich, I want to be rich. I don't want to look successful; I want to be successful. I don't want to look happy, I want to be happy. Feel your dreams. Be them. Don't just be all flash and no substance.

Everything starts with discovering your identity. If you don't know your identity, it will be impossible to know your calling and future. And if you don't know your value and worth, consider volunteering. Just start volunteering and working with your hands and mind, and you will quickly discover your strengths and develop the desires and passions that were already within you.

If you want to be rich, give. To become a leader, learn how to follow, volunteer, and serve. If you want to influence or be an influencer, be someone else's biggest groupie and supporter.

In this Discover phase, there are times to say yes, and there are times to say no. Initially, when you are discovering, say yes to everything. Try things out. Explore. But once you are in the development and deployment stages, then you begin to say no more and more.

There were two times in my life when I was between jobs. I had people asking me, multiple times, to work for them or at their company. I said no over and over. I believed it was because I was holding out for better positions.

But in reality, I was scared. I didn't know those fields, and didn't think I was prepared. But I eventually said yes. I dove in headfirst and learned as much as I could. I worked my way up, taking on more roles and assuming greater responsibility at each job. All because I said yes. However, as my plate became fuller, both at work and in life, I had to start saying no to more things, because I was already actively involved in the deployment process. Read on and you'll gain a deeper understanding.

You need to start making conscious decisions to achieve the best possible outcome of your goals. Dave Ramsey says you need to *"live like no one else, so you can live like no one else."* If you want to be better or different, you need to walk, talk, and think differently. Be the person you want to be now, even if it means losing friends or family along the way.

I have travelled for almost two decades of my life for work. And I found myself drinking a lot more and smoking on these work trips. I was out late for meetings or dinners. And if you're in New York or LA, you drink a little more, or party a little harder, and buy smokes from a random convenience store.

I didn't like who I became on work trips. I was compromising my values to fit in with colleagues. Drinking, smoking, and entertaining crude jokes at times. Making the decision to live with integrity everywhere, regardless of others' reactions, was uncomfortable but worth it for long-term character."

"If you think it's hard being successful, try being a failure."

- Brian Tracy

You need to remove "should", "could", and "want to" from your vocabulary. Replace them with "I can" and "I will".

And as Ed Mylett says, don't forget the power of the word *yet*. I'm not successful...**yet**. I'm not out of debt...**yet**. My business hasn't succeeded...**yet**. It reinforces your solutions to get there.

The Discover phase is also a phase of planning. As you discover and learn, you begin to assemble a skeletal framework of your goals and visions. God rewards plans. BUT...and that's a big but...never be so rigid and stuck in your plans that you're afraid to veer off course if the Lord says to, or if a new route opens up that is better or faster or more efficient. Proverbs 19:21 says, *"Many are the plans in a person's heart, but it is the Lord's purpose that prevails."* It's ok to plan for your future. But in the end, God is the ultimate veto and audible play caller.

In discovery, you learn as much as you can, preparing yourself for the next phase.

The 7 Mountains of Influence

I want to make something obvious. To be "called to the ministry" does NOT mean you need to be a pastor. Full stop. Being called to be a pastor is a very specific calling, NOT for everyone. But, we are ALL called to minister. There is a difference. There are a million areas in this world that need ministry, not just the four walls of a church.

1 Peter 2:9 says, "You are a chosen people, a royal priesthood, a holy nation, God's special possession, that you may declare the praises of him who called you out of darkness into his wonderful light."

Revelation 1:6 says, "and has made us to be a kingdom and priests to serve his God and Father—to him be glory and power for ever and ever! Amen."

Moses tells us in *Exodus 19:6* that, "you (we) will be a kingdom of priests and a holy nation."

Jesus's final words to us in *Matthew 28:19* were to "Go therefore and make disciples of all nations… teaching them to observe all that

I have commanded."

We are ALL called to minister. However, we are **NOT** all called to the ministry. Does that make sense?

Part of discovering your identity and your "why" is discovering your calling. What are you on this planet for? This spiritual foundation directly connects to what we'll explore in Part 2, when we discuss beginning with God.

"For the gifts and the calling of God are irrevocable."

- Romans 11:29

Paul tells us that before we were even born, Jesus placed gifts and callings into our lives, NEVER to be taken away. You have giftings you may not even know about. That's what's so fun about the discovery phase. As you build a closer relationship with God and learn more about your identity, you start to discover quirks or things you may have dismissed, and realize it's a God-given thing that should be used.

On the other hand, though, God may not take away those gifts, but He can remove your lampstand or influence. Your impact and influence directly correlate with your following God and using your gifts and talents for good.

Jesus tells us in Matthew 25 about the parable of the talents. The master goes on a journey and entrusts 3 servants with Talents. One with 5, another with 2, and the last with 1. The first two servants invest and double their original amount. The master praises them. He says, "Well done, good and faithful servant." But the third servant, acting out of fear and disobedience, hides his talent in the ground. He returns only the original amount and is rebuked. So much so that the master removes his influence and gives it to someone else who is more reliable and obedient.

Matthew 25:23 says, "Well done, good and faithful servant; you have been faithful over a few things, I will make you ruler over many things.

God wants to give you more. God wants to "expand your tent pegs." But He'll never do it if you aren't active in the faith and are not deploying out into His calling for your life.

Moral of the story: if you use what God gives you for His glory, you develop it, deploy it, and most importantly, you duplicate it. He will give you even more. But should you choose to hide your giftings or disobey God's calling, you'll lose it all.

> *"Your talent is God's gift to you. What you do with it is your gift back to God."*
>
> -   Leo Buscaglia

The 7 Mountains of Influence is a framework to help you narrow down your giftings and callings, providing an end goal for your journey. God has given you the gifts to climb these mountains, and overtake them. God is calling you to take back these mountains, to take back what He designed for us to have, going back to the Garden of Eden.

So what are the 7 Mountains? Take a "peak" below.

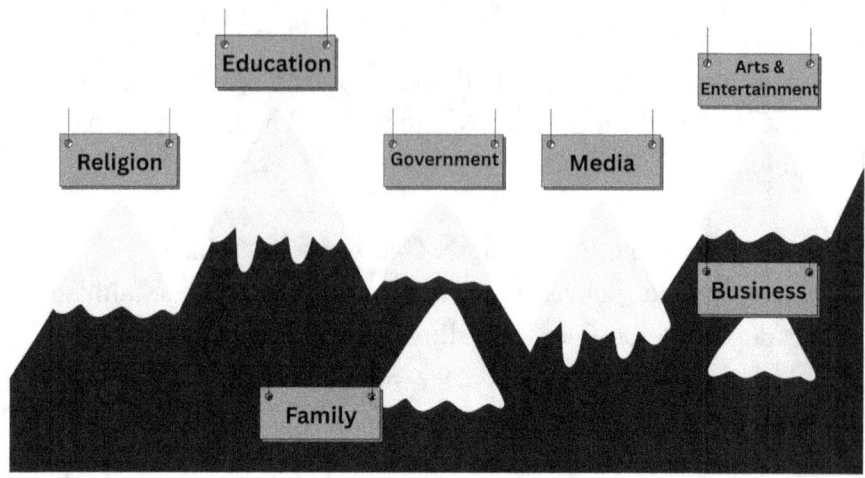

FAMILY

The family mountain involves marriage, parenting, and home life. This is the foundation for your values, identity, and generational legacy. This mountain needs to be fought for. This mountain lives not according to the world, but how God designed a family to be.

RELIGION

The religion mountain encompasses the church itself, its ministries, and even world religions, examining their impact. We are fighting for Christianity and the word of God. This mountain shapes your belief systems and moral foundations. If I'm being honest, this might be one of the quietest mountains, because the fear of the world and what they think is greater than our foundation and belief structure, as well as our resoluteness to defend it.

EDUCATION

The education mountain involves our schools, universities, and it's curriculum. It influences how truth, history, and identity are taught.

We are currently engaged in a significant battle for our children and the education they receive in public schools.

GOVERNMENT

The government mountain involves the law, politics, our nation and its local community leadership, and justice. It impacts how freedom, morality, and policy are upheld. We NEED more young Christian politicians in DC. We NEED more young Christian freedom fighters in local government. If we don't attack the government mountain, it'll only get worse.

MEDIA

The media mountain encompasses news, journalism, and, most notably, social media. The media mountain controls the narrative, spreads ideas, and either informs or misleads. This is why we need bright, young Christian minds in media, sharing the truth and the Gospel, and what is right and just. We need more Gospel content on TikTok and Instagram. We need more testimonies on Facebook. We need more teenagers unashamedly unafraid to post about Jesus. We need more parents, those Karens and Kens, to post about positive issues and not complaints and "what's wrong with the left." Social media isn't about being right; it's about being a light in a dark place.

ARTS & ENTERTAINMENT

The Arts & Entertainment mountain involves music, film, sports, books, and influencers. Think Hollywood, Nashville, New York, Las Vegas. This mountain shapes our culture, inspires imagination, and directs trends. Similar to the media mountain, this mountain has a profound hold on our younger generation. We need more of The Chosen and Angel Studios. We need more House of David and The Last Rodeo. We need agencies and studios to stop caring about being blacklisted and put their money where their mouth is, creating wholesome, Godly content, movies, and music. We need revival in CCM music and Nashville Christian music. We need fewer singular, egotistical pastors and more leaders who care about their sheep, instead of their egos and followers. If we had Christian leaders who are called to this mountain, focus more on God, we'd have less infidelity, affairs, and sexual sin. This mountain takes a special calling, because I believe this mountain has the single greatest temptation: money, drugs, sex, etc.

BUSINESS

The business mountain involves commerce, finance, and entrepreneurship. This mountain drives innovation, resources, and economic influence. What if you, as a wealthy business leader, invested more into younger entrepreneurs, instead of calling into Dave Ramsey with your baby step 7 numbers? What if you focused more on giving than getting? What if you dedicated your life to funding schools or businesses, or non-profits to help others take over the other six mountains? The business mountain is the fuel to many of the other mountains, because money makes things happen.

The idea is that cultural transformation happens when people of faith engage these areas with integrity, excellence, and the heart of God. Not to control them, but to bring truth, love, and positive influence. Yes, we want to be on top of the mountains, but we want it to be inclusive, not exclusive.

Now that you've identified your mountain of influence, you might be thinking, "This sounds overwhelming. How do I actually climb it?" That's where the development phase becomes crucial. You can't scale a mountain without proper preparation and training.
You're on the edge of something significant. Now that you've rediscovered your identity, chosen your purpose, and established

foundational habits, it's time to step into the deployment phase, moving beyond discovery to intentional development.

Let this chapter be your launchpad: from discovery to readiness, from private devotion to public impact. God is calling you, not just to find yourself, but to find your mountain and climb it, for His glory.

Now, let's start developing!

3. DEVELOP

The Develop phase is the investment phase. The practical application phase. This is really when you start working the system of habits, habit stacking. This is where you apply what you have learned in practice. This is an action step, but still mostly private.

"The best investment you can make is in yourself."

- Warren Buffett

There is only one you, and there's a good chance that many people will need you in some capacity at some point in your life. It's a disservice to others for you not to be living at your potential, to help as many people as possible.

As Napoleon Hill writes in Think and Grow Rich, "As knowledge is acquired, it must be organized and put into use, for a definite purpose, through practical plans. Knowledge has no value except that which can be gained from its application toward some worthy end."

Develop is where you start to apply what you've learned and take little steps forward. You start to try out a few new things. You try to implement a new habit or work to stop a bad one.

One of my favorite presidents ever, and one whom you'll be hearing many quotes from in this book, Teddy Roosevelt said, "The man who really counts in the world is the ***doer***, not the mere critic—the man who actually ***does*** the work, even if roughly and imperfectly, not the man who only talks or writes about how it ought to be done." You can discover all you want. You can take notes throughout the day. You can listen to podcasts until your ears bleed. But until you start DOING what you've discovered, you'll never grow an inch in your life.

James 1:22 says, *"But be doers of the word and not hearers only, deceiving yourselves."* Even James is telling you that there comes a time to stop talking and start walking. Do what is in your heart. Do what you already want to do. Start applying it now. It's time to stop planning and start doing. Take action on what you've learned.

The Development phase is the phase where you begin to master what you are practicing. This phase hurts sometimes. If you are starting weight training or exercising, you will literally and figuratively feel the effects as you apply your newfound knowledge. If you want to write a book, the hardest step is to sit down and start writing. But with every word, paragraph, and page, you become a stronger, more well-rounded writer. Frederick Douglass said, "If there is no struggle, there is no progress".

When I was going through my health (BODY) journey, I began rucking. Ruck just means walking with weight. I needed to get in shape, but running hurt because of the shock to my back and knees, and I'm not a heavyweight lifter. A guy from my men's group told us about how he rucks (and also had the same back surgery). Rucking supposedly burns three times as many calories as running, and it also benefits your back strength and core, as you have to utilize your muscles to maintain good posture while walking with the weight on your back. Rucking was a struggle at first. The weight, walking up and down big hills and trails. It wasn't pretty. The struggle was real. But so was the progress.

James 1:2-3 says, "Consider it pure joy, my brothers and sisters, whenever you face trials of many kinds, because you know that the testing of your faith produces perseverance." Consistency and perseverance only come through testing. You need to rewire your brain to become comfortable with being uncomfortable. Your brain naturally wants to stay in a comfortable state and avoid being challenged, but you will not persevere without testing, stretching yourself, and developing into a fierce warrior and agent of change.

The Three D's of Goal Setting

The Develop phase goes hand-in-hand with the Soul section in Part 5, where we'll explore the specific habits that transform your character and emotions. Sahil Bloom discusses ABC Goals in his book, The 5 Types of Wealth, a goal-setting method that we'll put into practice when we discuss habit formation in the Soul section.

Naturally, I've created this structure within the Four D's framework. I have another three D's for you. It's the **Three D's of Goal Setting.** This is a simple way to ensure you always make progress, regardless of your energy level.

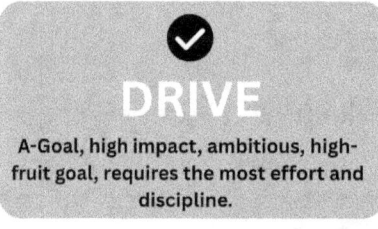

DRIVE

A-Goal, high impact, ambitious, high-fruit goal, requires the most effort and discipline.

DELIVER

B-Goal, medium impact, solid, reliable progress without as much pressure. Easily deliverable.

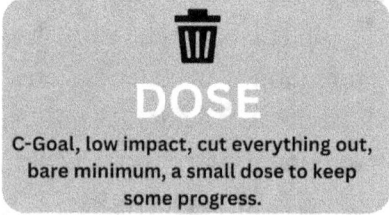

DOSE

C-Goal, low impact, cut everything out, bare minimum, a small dose to keep some progress.

DRIVE (A-Goal)

This is your high-octane target. It's the most ambitious goal you can accomplish when you have full-time energy. These are your high-impact, game-changing actions that get you the big wins. When you're firing on all cylinders, drive hard and go for maximum results.

DELIVER (B-Goal)

This is your steady progress target. It's realistic, dependable forward movement for normal days when life gets in the way. Deliver maintains momentum without overwhelming pressure. This is your "show up and do the work" level that keeps you consistently moving toward your goals.

DOSE (C-Goal)

This is your minimum viable action. For days when everything goes wrong, you're exhausted, or life is chaos - just take a small dose of progress. Even 30 seconds counts. This is your "anything above zero" goal that keeps the habit alive and you in the game.

The beauty of this system is that you always have a way forward. High energy days? Drive. Normal days? Deliver. Terrible days? Just take a dose. Consistency beats perfection, and anything above zero compounds over time.

For example, you won't always achieve your A goal on a daily basis. It's impossible. If you only aim for the highest goal, you will constantly live in defeat because you won't be able to do it every single day in every single moment. But still, set your A goal high. I want to work out for an hour a day.

Your B goal is when you're super tired, wake up late, the kids are being challenging, your spouse is upset, or a last-minute business meeting comes up, so you'll do a 20-30 minute walk.

And then your C goal is for those overwhelming days when you just need to get outside and soak up some sunshine for five minutes.

How to Apply the Three D's of Goal Setting

Here's how to put this system into practice across every area of your life:

Step 1: Set Your Three Levels. For any goal or habit (exercise, prayer time, business tasks, family time), create your three options:
- Drive Goal - Your peak performance target
- Deliver Goal - Your steady progress standard
- Dose Goal - Your bare minimum to stay in the game

Step 2: Match Your Energy to Your Level. Each day, honestly assess your capacity and choose accordingly:
- High energy and time? Go for Drive
- Normal day with typical constraints? Stick with Deliver
- Chaos, exhaustion, or overwhelm? Just take your Dose

Step 3: Always Do Something. The magic isn't in perfect execution - it's in never going to zero. Whether you Drive, Deliver, or Dose, you're building momentum. A two-minute prayer still counts. A five-minute walk still matters. One paragraph written still moves you forward.

This system transforms your goals from rigid expectations into flexible tools. Instead of failing when you can't hit your A-level target, you succeed by choosing the right level for your current reality.

Consistency in life, especially during the DEVELOP phase, is about doing something consistently. Consistency is like the faith of a mustard seed that grows into something huge. Remember, anything above zero compounds. Aim to Drive when you can, be proud to Deliver most days, and never feel guilty about taking just a Dose when that's all you've got.

The goal isn't perfection, it's persistence. Persistence always wins.

Consistency in DEVELOP Phase

What we think it means:

What it actually means:

Mark Twain hilariously said, "Quitting smoking is the easiest thing I've ever done. I've done it hundreds of times." Don't give up on your development. This is probably the phase where most dreams and goals die, because you're not strong enough to make it habitual or a career yet, and you're tired enough from trying that your energy is faint, and you can fall.

But here's what I've learned about the development process: real growth doesn't happen overnight, and it rarely looks impressive while it's happening. Let me share a powerful analogy that changed how I think about progress.

Bamboo vs Jet Ski

Look at the image above, and keep it in your mind as we continue.

In many parts of Asia, the Chinese bamboo tree is planted and watered like any other plant. But after planting the seed, nothing seems to happen for years. There is no visible growth. No sprout. Nothing breaks through the soil.

For five years, farmers water it, fertilize it, and protect the spot where it was planted. Then suddenly, in the fifth year, the bamboo tree shoots up to nearly 90 feet in just six weeks.

The truth is, during those five "silent" years, the bamboo was growing an underground root system strong enough to support the massive height it would eventually reach. Growth doesn't always feel fast or visible, especially when you're developing your character, faith, leadership, identity, giftings, or emotional maturity.

This growth, your development, takes time. Years even. But just like the bamboo, real growth happens beneath the surface before others see the results, and only if you don't quit!

Now look at the jetski. I heard it said that it is impossible to frown on a jet ski. But what does a jetski do? It skims the water. It's a "shallow" vehicle that only stays surface deep.

Being a bamboo farmer must be an awful, boring job. Tiresome and endless, until the breakthrough comes. But what if the farmer gave up in year four? He wouldn't see the reaping where he sowed. What if he quit in November of the fourth year, and that growth was about to pop in December? He'd miss out.

Contrast that again to the jet ski. It's fun, you're going fast, others are seeing your "success", you're living your best life. But it's only surface deep. There are no roots or foundation. You're just skimming the surface of what could be.

Growth takes time, and probably isn't that fun. To achieve true growth, it requires time, effort, and dedication.

Matthew 7:24-25 says, "Therefore whoever hears these sayings of Mine, and does them, I will liken him to a wise man who built his house on the rock: and the rain descended, the floods came, and the winds blew and beat on that house; and it did not fall, for it was founded on the rock."

If you build your foundation on the rock, your relationship with Jesus, growth becomes easier to achieve. Your determination not to quit will eventually see that 90 feet of growth in 6 weeks. Are you willing to invest 5 years of effort to see a significant growth explosion in a short amount of time?

Easy choices now often lead to a hard life later, and vice versa. Are you willing to overlook what's easy, to do what's right?

Distraction Doubt Dullness

The EVIL D's

The biggest enemy to the DEVELOP phase, and really any phase, is the EVIL D's. **Distraction**, **Doubt**, and **Dullness**.

Colossians 3:2 says, "Set your mind on things above, not earthly things." And just as Peter walked on water, as long as you stay focused on God, on the vision, on the plan, on the dream, on the goals, you may fall, but you will have the strength to get back up again and not succumb to defeat.

Distraction will take your eyes off the prize.
Doubt will cause fear to overtake you.
Dullness will cause you to lose motivation.

One hack to help avoid the evil D's is to introduce a consequence for failing to reach your goal. Many people don't take action because there isn't a consequence attached to it. If you want to lose 10 pounds, but have no negative consequences attached to not achieving that goal, if you start to get tired of working or quit, it's no big deal, because nothing happens if you quit.

But if you say, "I'm not going to Mexico for vacation this summer if I don't lose 10 pounds", then that added consequence will help you stay motivated to achieve your goal. Because if you don't, you'll miss out on a white sand beach vacation with tiki drinks.

The Bluey Methodology

I once heard someone joke that watching the show Bluey as a parent is almost depressing to watch because of how amazing Bandit and Chili are. They never falter. They're a rock, a perfect example of parenting. But think about it. Those episodes are about 5 minutes long. That's a 5-minute glimpse into their 24-hour day. You can't tell me Bandit doesn't finish work or get done putting them to bed, and just wants time alone to watch a game. Don't tell me Chili doesn't sneak a sip of wine after dealing with a visit from Muffin and the loudness that house must be.

All that to say this. It doesn't matter how bad your day is. It doesn't matter how much you miss the mark. It doesn't matter if you barely hit your C-goals the entire week. EVERYONE has a good 5 minutes in them. No one is perfect. Get your 5 minutes of Bluey joy in your life, and aim for 10 minutes the next day.

Now that you've been refined in the quiet places, it's time to show up in the public spaces.

You've trained in the shadows, now step into the light. You've built the habits, now it's time to build impact.

Let's go! It's time to DEPLOY.

4. DEPLOY

The Deploy phase is the phase where practice becomes a habit. This is where the application becomes an occupation. These habits are now ingrained in you. They're part of your DNA. Everything you've learned and discovered, planned and developed is now your "occupation". It's part of your identity. You went from "I want to be wealthy" to "I am wealthy". You went from "I want to lose 20 pounds" to "I am 25 pounds down and feel great!" These types of transformations we'll explore practically in our Body and Soul sections. Or at least you're close to it, but close enough to where you can begin to focus on other things while still maintaining it.

Think of the Deploy phase like the army. You are only deployed after completing basic training. You need to be ready for the war ahead. If you deploy too early, before you're ready, you will be destined to fail.

Or think of your favorite sports team. Mine is the Oregon Ducks college football team. Think about it. If they just practiced...all day long...all season long, but never entered the game, what's the point? They'll put in all that work developing themselves, but never deploy and be in a position to win the game. But once they're ready, they take the field and they beat Michigan and Ohio State to win their 1st Big 10 conference undefeated in their very first season. Go Ducks!

James 2:17 says, "Faith without works is dead." Works and "doing" do NOT get you into Heaven, and they certainly have no bearing on your salvation as the reason. But, works DO prove your faith. There comes a point where just hearing and preparing is no longer enough; you have to act. Deploying is setting your faith in motion. The hope is what your end goal is. Faith will lead you there, but only if you take steps.

"You don't have to be great to start, but you have to start to be great."

\- Zig Ziggler

The four D's are designed to take you through every stage of growth. Ultimately, the goal of our lives is to be who God has called us to be, and to walk in the gifts and callings, favor, and grace that He wants to pour out on us and through us. We just need to decide to step out onto the field and play. Discover and Develop are minor leagues. Deploy moves you up into the big leagues. This is your money maker.

I've lived most of my life for other people. I was promoted in my career very early and worked my way up at almost every company I worked for. But, I did it for status and to appear successful. I have made decisions based on other people, or not made decisions, out of fear of how they would react. Again, I looked put together, but didn't feel it. The third and fourth D's were my stumbling blocks. There was a vast canyon between Develop and Deploy. In one of those steps, there is safety. The other involves action.

As you move into the Deploy and Duplicate phases, you'll begin to see signs that you've found your soul purpose in life, which might include feeling a sense of alignment, peace, and fulfillment. You may also notice that your actions feel more meaningful and that you're naturally drawn towards activities that resonate with your inner values and contribute to your spiritual growth.

Your life's trajectory is composed of tiny moments and decisions that compound and build up over time. You win some and you lose some. But the key is consistency. Consistency is not winning 100%

of the time; it's about finishing the game when you're tired, failing, and defeated.

I heard someone mention a quote on a podcast, and it has stuck with me for several years now. Ready, FIRE, aim. Yes, you read that correctly. Discover and Develop is the readying phase. You're preparing for battle, getting your ducks in a row, packing your supplies, crossing your i's and dotting your t's.

Deploy means to FIRE! You know what to do now. You have the knowledge. You have the practice. Now just start firing. The aim will follow soon after. Open a business, launch a podcast, start a ministry, write a book. Just start firing at anything your ambition and heart are telling you to. Once you start hitting, your aim will catch up. It's a weird, backwards quote, but it rings true.

> *"Do not wait; the time will never be 'just right.' Start where you stand..."*
>
> - Napoleon Hill

Psalm 127:4 says, "Children are like arrows in the hands of a warrior." Similarly, your giftings and callings are like those same arrows. Your life mission is meant to be released and shot forth!

Most people are afraid to take action because they are scared of making the wrong decision. Successful people make a decision, and then make it right.

> *"Just Freaking Do It!"*
>
> - Dan Martell

Our trusty podcast host Ed Mylett said, "Our obsession becomes our possession." Too often, we obsess over what we don't have or over our fears. And when those negative things run our lives, we will never achieve the success or the dreams we want.

The DEPLOY phase is a phase of *sacrifice or surrender*. Sacrifice whatever it takes to get to where God is calling you, and to achieve the dreams and visions that you feel are from him.

"Surrender is not about giving up, it's about giving more power to where it really belongs."

You're not a little boy or little girl anymore. The DEPLOY phase is a grown-up, mature, adulting phase that requires mature decision-making. You need to sacrifice everything — **except your family**. That's one thing I refuse to negotiate. Never sacrifice a sports game or being there to put them to bed. There are, of course, exceptions to the rule. However, ensure that they are 100% exceptions, and never let it become the rule to miss family time.

I've worked from home a majority of my adult career, and I've always made a point to "shut off" at 5:00 pm. 5-7 is always family time. My wife is a stay-at-home mom, and she gets her evening therapy and time away from the kids, which she enjoys, including cooking dinner.

So, I take over with the kids at 5, and from 5-7 pm we do family time, dinner AT THE TABLE (I can't stress the importance of this enough), bathtime, our evening episodes of Curious George, rice cakes, and bedtime. We don't do screens during this time. 5-7 also happens to be the witching hours for my kids, so it ain't easy. But again, this is the sacrifice I make to have family time over anything else. After the kids are in bed, I can check emails or texts, or continue writing or creating content.

Learning how to balance family and work life is a key role of the Deploy phase. You can't be a leader in business or church or in the marketplace if you aren't a leader at home. Balance is key, but don't be under the illusion that you can separate them entirely. You have to intertwine family and work. You have to as a business owner. There will be times my kids or my wife travel with me. Everyone will adjust to that pace of life.

Let's Talk About Boats

I heard a sermon a long time ago that I've always held onto. And I've applied one of my all-time favorite songs ever to it. But, there are four reasons why someone may not move into the deployment phase.

1. *You're still in the harbor* because of weariness, and you thought parking your boat would be the restful thing to do. A ship in the harbor is safe, but it's not what a ship was built for. A ship is built to deploy on a voyage.

2. *Our anchors are down* and are anchored to hurts from our past.

Philippians 3:13 says, "I do not consider myself yet to have taken hold of it. But one thing I do: Forgetting what is behind and straining toward what is ahead." You must forget all past failures and hurts in order to sail towards your future.

3. *Your rudder is working in the wrong direction*, against what god is doing or where His wind is blowing you. James 3 talks about your tongue being the rudder of a ship, and that we say will direct our path. As your rudder speaks, so will your ship steer.

4. *Our sails aren't raised* to catch the prophetic flow. When things aren't happening, we take down our sails cause it hasn't happened yet, we get tired of waiting.

II Thessalonians 3:13 says, "But as for you, brethren, do not grow weary in doing good." Don't lose faith. Don't quit. Keep sailing!

I will sail my vessel
'Til the river runs dry
Like a bird upon the wind
These waters are my sky
I'll never reach my destination
If I never try
So I will sail my vessel
'Til the river runs dry

- Garth Brooks, the River

***"Ships are safest in the harbor — but that's not what ships
are built for."***

- William G.T. Shedd

Imagine these two ships:

One sits in the harbor. Shining, untouched, perfectly maintained. The other returns from a long journey. It is scarred, sails torn, hull worn from salt and storm.

One has **no** stories.

The other has legends, lives saved, goods delivered, and maps rewritten.

Which ship fulfilled its purpose? Which ship are you?

Again, you can choose what is easy and safe. Your ship will look immaculate. Or you can set sail, be battered by the wind and the waves, make it through storm after storm, have a dirty, beaten-up ship, but on an island of success, wealth, potential, fortune, and legacy.

45

So here you are; deployed. You've left the harbor. Your ship is moving. The habits you once had to force now flow. The calling you once questioned now compels you. You're in motion, and that motion is changing everything.

But now comes the most powerful part of all. What if this journey wasn't just for you? What if everything you've learned, become, and battled through... was meant to be reproduced in others?

The final phase of growth isn't just achievement, it's multiplication. It's when your breakthrough becomes someone else's starting point. It's when you realize the legacy isn't in what you've done, but in who you raise up to go further.

Deploy is about doing the work. Duplicate is about developing the worker.

Let's talk about that.

5. DUPLICATE

Duplicate is the multiplication phase. It's the making disciples that makes disciples phase. It's the hand-off phase. The legacy phase. You've taken all you've discovered, developed, and deployed in the first three D's, and are paying it forward to someone else. Pouring what could, and should, be years of life into another person that you are mentoring and discipling.

The Duplicate phase is writing a book for others to learn and grow. This phase involves starting a podcast about leadership, church, family, or business, for others to listen to and be inspired. This phase involves weekly coffee with a younger person (or an older one) and mentoring them through their life's problems and/or victories.

The Duplicate phase is the best and final part of the Great Commission itself. Matthew 28:19-20 says, "Go therefore and make disciples of all the nations, baptizing them in the name of the Father and of the Son and of the Holy Spirit, teaching them to observe all things that I have commanded you."

Our mission in life, or in our family, or in our business, should be to see souls saved and disciples made. We need to make disciples. We need to pass on our knowledge, experience, and lessons learned to the next generation of leaders. It is our life's missional meaning to make disciples. So if we aren't duplicating what we've done in the first three D's, then we're wasting a whole lot of time, energy, and potential.

John Mark Comer asks these questions in his book Practicing the

Way. I've added the Jessee spin on some, too.

Who are you following?
Who is following you?
Who are you discipling?
Who is discipling you?

The truth is, you are ALL following someone. Is that person or network, or podcast leading you to deeper growth and relationships, or is it pushing you away?

We are ALL discipling someone. We lead by example, and someone is always watching. So, who do you think is being discipled by you? By your actions? By your speech and "content" you put out?

You've heard, "you can lead a horse to water but you can't make him drink." That is true. However, we can do everything in our power to lead the horse to the water.

Jesus didn't call us to be Christians; he called us to follow. To come under him and be discipled. His entire life was an example of what it means to be discipled (His relationship with the Father) and to disciple others.

The Spirit of Elijah

Malachi 4:5-6 says, "I will send you Elijah the prophet. Before the coming of the great and dreadful day of the Lord. And he will turn the hearts of the fathers to the children, and the hearts of the children to their fathers."

The Spirit of Elijah is one of the most impactful, multiplying, and duplicative theologies in the Bible. Its power is unparalleled in making disciples who, in turn, make disciples.

This verse is about generational reconciliation and revival, often interpreted as a symbol of God's desire to restore the family structure and heal generational divides before His return. However, the idea is that what begins with personal deployment should ultimately flow outward to family, to disciples, and to the next generation. It is exactly what Elijah's spirit represents: not just power, but preparation for legacy.

Renowned Atheist Penn Jillette once said in an interview, "I've always said that I don't respect people who don't proselytize. I don't respect that at all. If you believe that there's a heaven and a hell, and people could be going to hell or not getting eternal life, and you think that it's not really worth telling them this because it would make it socially awkward—and atheists who think people shouldn't proselytize and who say just leave me along and keep your religion to yourself—how much do you have to hate somebody to not proselytize? How much do you have to hate somebody to believe everlasting life is possible and not tell them that?"

Wow! Someone who doesn't even believe in God has more respect for God fearing people who share about God than those who don't. That should wake up a lot of you. We need to disciple, to proselytize, to duplicate our very being as much as we can. Other people's lives depend on you. And if you don't graduate from the Deploy phase to Duplicate, a lot of people will miss out on your gifting.

If you think you have the answer to life and death, hell and the grave, shame on us for not sharing it with everyone. Or if you think you have a cure for cancer, the latest autism breakthrough, church development, or fill-in-the-blanks, and you don't let the world see it, take it, and make it better, then your life is just a shadow of the greatness God has called you to.

I hope that last paragraph wasn't too jarring. However, I want to emphasize the importance of duplication and discipleship in our lives. Future generations can't afford for us to sit and wait, not passing on our gifts, businesses, or family wisdom. You are uniquely qualified to help the person you used to be.

> *"People don't care how much you know, until they know how much you care."*

> *-   Teddy Roosevelt*

This quote from Teddy is my life's mantra. It's the foundation on which I build my relationships with my wife, my kids, my friends, my colleagues, and the strangers I meet at the gas station. Paul says in 1 Corinthians 4:15, "For though you might have ten thousand instructors in Christ, yet you do not have many fathers." How true is this?

Look at social media. We have ten times ten thousand "teachers". Everyone knows the answer or has something to say. The keyboard warriors are never short of advice, yet they remain silent when it comes to criticizing others. True leaders, mentors, disciple-makers, fathers, and mothers take time to build relationships and rapport. They invest emotional and physical energy in listening to and guiding people. They show people it's not about what they know, it's about how much they care. Then the benefit of building that trust is that you can share what you know. Win-win.

Once you care enough about yourself to make these changes, you should care enough about your friends and family, and everyone else, to share them.

The key to successful leadership and discipleship is influence, not authority. It's relationships, not fear. Influence is fueled by love, not power.

1 Corinthians 13:1 says, "Though I speak with the tongues of men and of angels, but have not love, I have become sounding brass or a clanging cymbal." Leadership without love is brash and harsh. Leadership and discipleship without love and relationship will falter and break. However, if you establish a sense of "relational equity" with people, duplication is likely to occur.

> *"You can count the seeds in an apple, but you can't count the apples in a seed."*
>
> \- Karen Jensen

When we duplicate ourselves into others, we're not just adding, we're multiplying. One faithful disciple can create hundreds of ripple effects you may never see. A "family tree" of disciple making disciples. A legacy of trees.

It's not just multiplication either. It's exponential.

Leviticus 26:8 says, "Five of you will chase a hundred, and a hundred of you will chase ten thousand, and your enemies will fall by the sword before you."

Matthew 18:20 says, "For where two or three are gathered together in My name, I am there in the midst of them."

There is power in many. There is power in community. There is power in duplication. And when you are walking in the fullness of your calling and identity, God can multiply your impact and influence exponentially.

> *"There is no problem in human life that apprenticeship to Jesus cannot solve."*
>
> \- Dallas Willard

The Duplicate phase isn't just the final step; it's the fruit-bearing proof that the other three D's worked. Discover, Develop, and

Deploy were never meant to end with you. They were meant to flow through you into others. Legacy doesn't happen by accident; it happens by intention. Discipleship is not a suggestion. It's a commission. And your influence, multiplied through relationships, mentorship, and bold obedience, will outlast your timeline.

You are a seed with the potential to grow an orchard. So don't let your wisdom die with you. Pass it on. Write the book. Mentor the teen. Launch the podcast. Take the coffee meeting. Start the group. Lead with love. Walk in truth. You are uniquely qualified to help the person you used to be, and someone out there is waiting for the version of you who obeyed the call to Duplicate.

Renew4D Reflection: The Four D's - Your Roadmap to Renewal

Discover the lie you've believed.

You've believed transformation had to be dramatic, instant, or "original." You thought you had to reinvent the wheel to grow. You believed your past roles or performances defined your future purpose. However, the truth is that real change is built through small habits and daily alignment. What you need is not a new framework. It's the discipline to live out one that works.

Develop truth statements rooted in God's Word.

- "If anyone is in Christ, he is a new creation." – 2 Corinthians 5:17
- "For as a man thinks in his heart, so is he." – Proverbs 23:7
- "Be doers of the word, and not hearers only." – James 1:22
- "Go and make disciples of all nations..." – Matthew 28:19

These truths ground the Four D's in both identity and action. Knowing who you are, then taking action.

Deploy daily habits that strengthen mental and spiritual resilience.

The Four D's are not just a concept—they're a lifestyle strategy:

- *Discover* your identity, calling, and purpose through journaling, prayer, and reflection.
- *Develop* those discoveries into new habits and disciplines. Start applying what you learn—imperfectly but consistently.
- *Deploy* your gifts in the real world. Take the risk. Launch the thing. Say yes to the call.
- *Duplicate* your growth by pouring into others. Start

mentoring, discipling, and teaching what you've learned through your own experiences.

Use this every day in every area: body, soul, mind, spirit.
Write it. Speak it. Live it. Repeat it.

Duplicate this mindset shift in others by modeling and mentoring.

Don't hoard your transformation. Share your story. Hand off the playbook. Pour into others the way someone once poured into you. Be the leader, the friend, the parent, or the spouse who multiplies. Use your Renew4D identity to empower others to find theirs. And remember, you are uniquely qualified to help the person you used to be.

Section Wrap-Up: Review & Reflection

What did you DISCOVER about the Four D's?

_____

_____

_____

_____

What will you begin to DEVELOP with the Four D's?

_____

_____

_____

_____

What will you DEPLOY in your life using the Four D's?

_____

_____

_____

_____

What will DUPLICATE and teach someone else about the Four D's?

_____

_____

_____

_____

CELEBRATION TIME

You just mastered the complete roadmap to life transformation! You've learned the Four D's framework that can be applied to any goal, habit, or dream in your life. You now understand how to Discover your identity and calling, Develop new skills through consistent practice, Deploy your gifts publicly with courage, and Duplicate your transformation by mentoring others. Most importantly, you've discovered that you don't need a new framework—you need the discipline to live out one that works, and you now have that system.

Put this book down and take action on your first D right now. Choose one area of your life and start in the Discover phase—research, pray, journal about it. Tell someone about the 7 Mountains of Influence and which mountain you feel called to climb. Share your biggest breakthrough from learning the Four D's framework. Remember, you are uniquely qualified to help the person you used to be, and this system will get you there.

Don't put off being happy for the sake of growing and grinding.

PART 2

THE SPIRIT

6. SPIRIT: BEGIN WITH GOD (SHEMA)

I recently published a devotional book called The 160 Day Journey (*shameless plug; available on all major book-buying sites, both physical and digital*). This devotional was born in the quiet early mornings of 2020-2021, when I finally found a way to strip away the noise and hear God's voice again.

The 160-Day Journey began not with confidence, but with conviction, a prompting from the Holy Spirit to stop amplifying fear and start speaking life. It began during the chaos of the COVID-19 pandemic, but what emerged was far more lasting: a deeper walk with God and a Renew4D spirit.

My finances were in shambles, and due to the pandemic, my company reduced my salary by half, forcing me to find a second (and even third) job to help make ends meet. The devotional was born while cleaning floors and toilets at a Christian academy.

Each morning became an altar. A chance to reset. To remember that I didn't need to have it all together. I just needed to show up. That's still true today. You don't need perfection to start walking with purpose. You just need presence. God's presence first, your full presence next.

We've all faced uncertainty. But through Jesus, we have a solid foundation and a faithful promise: "He will not let you be tested beyond what you can bear... He will provide a way of escape" (1 Corinthians 10:13 TPT). My hope was never in headlines, vaccines, or control—it was (and still is) anchored in something far greater.

The journey of spiritual renewal starts with making your spirit the lead voice in your day. Not your schedule. Not your social feed. Not your fear. When the Spirit leads, the rest of you, mind, body, and soul, find alignment.

Your spirit is where all true renewal begins. It's your direct connection to God and the foundation that determines the health of every other area in your life. Without a Renew4D spirit, you're building on sand; everything else will eventually crumble.

How the 4 D's Apply to Your Spirit:

DISCOVER: Your true identity in Christ and God's calling on your life

DEVELOP: Daily spiritual disciplines like prayer, Scripture study, and worship

DEPLOY: Walking in your God-given purpose and spiritual gifts

DUPLICATE: Making disciples and passing on your spiritual growth to others

Why Your Spirit Matters for Renewal:

Your spirit isn't just one part of life; it's the power source for all of it. When your spirit is aligned with God, your mind finds peace, your soul discovers purpose, and your body becomes the temple it was designed to be. Every other area of renewal flows from this foundation.

What You'll Accomplish:

By the end of this section, you'll have established a daily rhythm of connecting with God, learned to hear His voice clearly, and discovered how to let your spirit lead your decisions instead of your circumstances, emotions, or fears.

Let's begin where the world began. With the Word.

John 1:1 says, "In the beginning was the Word, and the Word was with God, and the Word was God." The foundation of the world started with the word. These words, "let there be light." So this is where I want you to start your journey to Renewal.

Paul says in Galatians 5:25, "If we live in the Spirit, let us also walk in the Spirit." If we walk in the spirit and pray in the spirit, we effectively have an unlimited source of spiritual nutrition, energy, and power; we have our offense and our defense. But it all starts with our special sauce, something that should be a daily ritual and prayer.

It's called the **_Shema_**, which in Hebrew means "listen".

Deuteronomy 6:4-9 - "Hear, O Israel: The Lord our God, the Lord is one! You shall love the Lord your God with all your heart, with all your soul, and with all your strength. "And these words which I command you today shall be in your heart. You shall teach them diligently to your children, and shall talk of them when you sit in your house, when you walk by the way, when you lie down, and when you rise up. You shall bind them as a sign on your hand, and they shall be as frontlets between your eyes. You shall write them on the doorposts of your house and on your gates.

Mark 12:28-30 - "Then one of the scribes came, and having heard them reasoning together, perceiving that He had answered them well, asked Him, "Which is the first commandment of all?" Jesus answered him, "The first of all the commandments is: 'Hear, O Israel, the Lord our God, the Lord is one. And you shall love the Lord your God with all your heart, with all your soul, with all your mind, and with all your strength.' This is the first commandment."

In the opening section of Deuteronomy, where this famous prayer first appears, Moses addresses the new generation of Israel as they prepare to enter the Promised Land. He is urging them not to repeat the mistakes of their parents' generation, wanting them to experience the full blessing of the promised land. But to do so, the people must learn to listen to and love God fully, above all else.

Listen

The opening line, "Hear, O Israel," does not simply mean to let sound waves enter your ears. Here, the word shema means to allow the words to sink in, provide understanding, and generate a response. It's about action. In Hebrew, hearing and doing are the same thing.

That's why so many Psalms start with "listen"; the author wants God to actively pay attention and respond to his cry.

What's the difference between hearing and listening?

There is a difference between hearing and listening. You can hear me speaking and get nothing, but if you truly listen, you'll receive, retain, grow, and DO. Listen to God. Listen when you read the bible. Don't just read, study. The more you learn to be in His presence, the more you will listen more intently, which will grow your spirit exponentially.

Carl Anderson writes an amazing book called ***Love Speaks***, in which he outlines 21 powerful ways to recognize God's multi-faceted voice. Each method is biblically backed and rooted in both Scripture and real-life experience, showing that God is not silent. He is constantly speaking. From the still small voice to dreams, visions, nature, and even divine appointments, Anderson reveals just how creative and personal God's communication can be. The question isn't whether God is speaking. The real question is, are we paying attention? Are we truly listening to what He is saying?

Love

The next instruction in the prayer is to love the Lord your God. What we translate into English as "love" here is the Hebrew word ahavah. Ahavah is not about the warm, fuzzy, emotional energy we feel when we like someone. It's not saying "I love Peyton Manning, or Clyde Drexler". Much like listening, biblical love is about action. You ahavah someone when you act in loyalty and faithfulness. For Israel, loving means faithful obedience to God.

This prayer is about listening to and loving God. But the prayer continues, "you shall love the Lord your God with all your heart, with all your soul, and with all your strength." In other words, people are to love God with all their being. Their knowledge, their existence, everything that they are is to love God with action, obedience, and covenant faithfulness. To have a right spirit means to love God.

Deuteronomy 10:12-13 - "And now, Israel, what does the Lord your God require of you, but to fear the Lord your God, to walk in all His ways and to love Him, to serve the Lord your God with all your heart and with all your soul, and to keep the commandments of the Lord and His statutes which I command you today for your good?"

God requires obedience and faithfulness, but above all...love. Get your spirit right and increase your faith...through loving God and others.

Heart

The heart is an amazing thing. The heart feels deeply and can hold a great deal of emotion. The Hebrews at one time had no understanding of the brain or a term to describe it, so they believed that all intellect originated from the heart. You know with your heart, your heart holds understanding. Proverbs says wisdom dwells in the heart. Solomon uses his heart to discern between good and evil. The heart holds feelings, physicality, emotions, fear, distress, pain...but also joy. Have a heart of joy. The heart is where you make choices motivated by your desires. Your affections and desires come from the heart.

That's why it says, 'Guard your heart.'

Proverbs 4:23 - Guard your heart, because from it flows your whole life.

- Moses said that to love god truly, your heart must be circumcised, which is a very grown-up analogy for removing something that's not needed, evil, and stubbornness from the human heart.
- David, after he commits adultery, asks God to create in me a clean heart.
- Ezekiel asked God to remove the heart of stone from the people and give them a new heart of flesh.
- Jeremiah asked God to write His laws on the hearts of men.

In the bible, the heart is at the very center of your being and existence. You are hopefully now seeing the importance of your relationship with God being the foundation of a Renew4D life. Your spirit guides your daily emotions, actions, and thoughts. Having a right heart and love only fuels the spiritual fire.

Strength

The Hebrew word is me'od...which doesn't mean just strength, but VERY or MUCH strength. It's a word that comes beside. God calls the world he made me'od good. Noah, when the flood waters rose, the storm became me'od powerful. Cain wasn't just angry at Abel; he was me'od angry. When Saul became king of Israel, he was me'od happy. Me'od intensifies the meaning of another word, increasing the force of a word. This isn't strength in the sense of muscle power, but rather a different kind of power.

So love god with all your heart (will and affections), soul (whole life and physical being), and strength or me'od (with muchness). Loving God with all your me'od means devoting every possibility, opportunity, and capacity that you have to honoring god and loving your neighbor as yourself.

Renewal starts by listening deeply, loving actively, and aligning completely with God. It's about letting your spirit become the first voice you respond to each day—and making that voice anchored in the Word.

Anchoring the devotional is the idea that spiritual renewal begins by letting your spirit lead. Not your schedule, your fear, or your newsfeed—but your spirit. When your spirit is aligned with God, everything else (mind, body, soul) begins to fall into place.

Renew4D Reflection: Let Your Spirit Lead

Discover the lie you've believed.

You've believed that you need to have it all together to walk in purpose. That perfection is a prerequisite for progress. That chaos in the world means chaos in your life. But that's not true. The truth is: you just need to show up. God's presence first. Your full presence next.

Develop truth statements rooted in God's Word.

- "It is written: In the beginning was the Word." (John 1:1)
- "It is written: If we live in the Spirit, let us also walk in the Spirit." (Galatians 5:25)
- "It is written: Love the Lord your God with all your heart, soul, mind, and strength." (Mark 12:30)

Deploy daily habits that strengthen mental and spiritual resilience.

Create a morning routine. Before the noise, before the news, before the pressure. Listen to God through His Word. Practice the Shema with the intention of listening to obey. Read slowly. Pray intentionally. Love actively. Let your spirit set the tone for your day, and everything else, mind, body, and soul, will align in power.

Duplicate this mindset shift in others by modeling and mentoring.

Tell the real story. Share how you met God not at the mountaintop, but scrubbing floors. Show others that it's not about status. It's about surrender. Teach your kids, your friends, your team what it means to love God with all your me'od; with all your muchness. That's how revival starts. One Renew4D spirit at a time.

7. SPIRIT: GET IT IN YOU

One of the most famous wilderness experiences in the Bible is when Jesus went into the wilderness for 40 days and fasted, and was tempted by the devil, as recorded in Matthew 4:1-11.

How did Jesus defeat the devil? He beat the devil and temptation with three simple words.

It. Is. Written.

The ONLY way to defeat the enemy is by the word of god. Struggling with peer pressure...it is written. Struggling with depression or anxiety...it is written. We'll explore how this biblical truth transforms your thought patterns in Part 4, with a focus on mind renewal. Struggling with porn or lust...it is written. Struggling in a lifeless marriage...it is written. In the middle of a mid-life crisis...IT IS WRITTEN!

James 1:22 - "But be doers of the word, and not hearers only, deceiving yourselves."

If Jesus had merely read scripture, or attended church on Sundays, or every men's breakfast, but never practiced what He learned, He would never have had the authority to turn away the devil.

So why am I saying all of this?

What I hope for you, both during and after reading this book, is that you will walk away with a deeper relationship with God. To truly KNOW Him more. I want to see you walk away set free from sin and addiction, encouraged and shown true love by Almighty God, healed emotionally and mentally, walking in power, and Renew4D in the spirit!

Joshua 1:8 - "This Book of the Law shall not depart from your mouth, but you shall meditate in it day and night, that you may observe to do according to all that is written in it. For *then* you will make your way *prosperous*, and then you will have *good success*.

If you're reading this book, you're probably at a crossroads. Maybe you're in your 40s, wondering 'Is this it?' Perhaps you're in your 20s, feeling stuck in someone else's plan or wanting to break out of the collegiate cycle and launch into something entrepreneurial. Perhaps you're anywhere in between, just knowing there has to be more.

If you don't study the word and get it in you, you will never reach your full potential, nor have the "firepower" to overcome adversity.

Matthew 22:37 - "Jesus said to him, 'You shall love the Lord your God with all your heart, with all your soul, and with all your mind.'"

We can deduce from all of this that the only way to truly live a Renew4D life and overcome sin, temptation, and adversity is by reading, studying, and applying the Word.

Your journey starts now. Or the following morning, after reading this chapter. You need to start a new morning routine. You need to get in the habit of going to God first. Starting your day with God, in His Word, and His presence. The famous song says it best: "In the morning when I rise, give me Jesus."

Isaiah 50:4 - "Morning by morning he awakens; he awakens my ear to hear."

Mark 1:35 - "Very early in the morning, while it was still dark, Jesus got up, left the house and went off to a solitary place, where he prayed."

Luke 5:16 - "But he would withdraw to deserted places and pray."

There's a reason the bible is littered with scripture showing how Jesus goes to a quiet place in the mornings to pray and be with God. So why shouldn't we do the same? If you want your spirit to be Renew4D, you need to be with the one who can help you achieve it.

It's about relationships. The more time you spend with someone, the stronger that relationship gets. If you don't spend time with God, how do you expect to hear his voice in times of trial and stress? How do you expect to be gung-ho for the Four D's and taking back your life, body, soul, mind...if your spirit is weak and malnourished?

Can you have faith without hope?

Think about that for a second.

Hebrews 11:1 says, "Faith is the substance of things hoped for, the evidence of things not seen." How can you have faith without hope? You can't. You need to have hope in something in order to have faith that takes its place until you achieve or receive it.

Let's say you're hoping to get out of debt and become financially free. That hope is the vision of a future you want. No more collectors, a paid-off house, freedom to give generously. But you don't see it yet. *Faith is what bridges the gap between where you are and where you believe God is taking you.* Faith looks like making a budget, trusting God with your tithe, applying for a job you feel underqualified for, and saying "no" to the impulse to add to your

Amazon cart. It's an action based on a hope that hasn't happened yet.

Hope gives you the picture; faith does the walking.

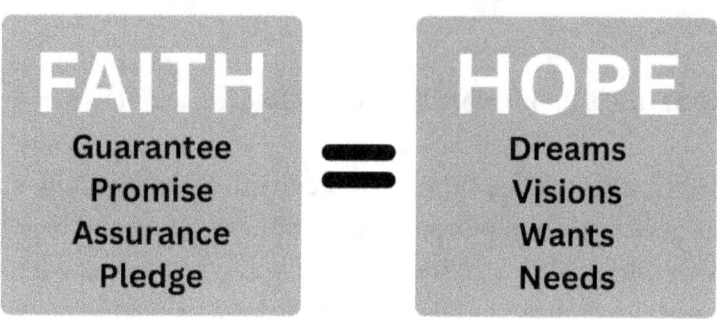

Now, let's take a mid-chapter brain break.

What are you HOPING to get out of reading this book?

_____

_____

_____

_____

What are you HOPING to change?

_____

_____

_____

_____

If you don't have any hope, it is impossible to have faith. If you have no faith, then it is impossible to grow in your relationship with God. It's a time to start hoping again. It's time to start dreaming again. What have you lost hope in? Where has your faith wavered? Are there things you've always wanted to do, but never did them, or were you too afraid to step out into the discomfort of entrepreneurship?

This first area of life needs renewal. You need to increase your faith by hoping again. A new job. A better marriage. Starting a business and being debt-free. Hope...and your faith will follow. As faith follows, your spirit will soar to new heights. As all of that increases, your relationship with God HAS to strengthen.

He is good, and good things will follow good things even more. Consider this a faith stack. Level up, from faith to faith. Faith for a job turns into faith for being debt-free, which in turn leads to starting your own business, buying your family's dream home, and hosting a Super Bowl party to show off your amazing patio, pool, and grill. But if your spirit isn't right...this is all just a sad pipedream.

The spirit is the spark of life and the seat of identity. It's where true transformation begins. In the Renew4D journey, your spirit is the part of you that connects directly with God. It's your inner compass, your eternal core, and the source of renewal that shapes every other area: body, soul, and mind.

When your spirit is made alive in Christ, everything else finds order. It's not about self-help or hustle. It's about surrender. Through prayer, purpose, and presence, your spirit becomes the lamp of the Lord (***Proverbs 20:27***), revealing who you are and why you're here.

Your spirit isn't one part of life. It's the power source for all of it.

Renew4D Reflection: "It. Is. Written."

Discover the lie you've believed.

You've believed that willpower, performance, or hustle are enough to defeat the battles in your mind. That success will prove your worth or that your spiritual life is separate from your daily grind. The truth? Without the Word, you have no weapon. Without the Spirit, you have no power.

Develop truth statements rooted in God's Word.
- "It is written: I am more than a conqueror through Him who loves me." (Romans 8:37)
- "It is written: I am not alone. God will never leave me nor forsake me." (Hebrews 13:5)
- "It is written: I have the mind of Christ." (1 Corinthians 2:16)
- "It is written: Man shall not live by bread alone, but by every word that proceeds from the mouth of God." (Matthew 4:4)

Deploy daily habits that strengthen mental and spiritual resilience.

Start every morning the Jesus way: in silence, with Scripture, and in prayer. Build your altar in the early hours. Speak Scripture out loud. Use your mouth to declare what your mind needs to believe. Don't just read the Bible. Wield it.

Duplicate this mindset shift in others by modeling and mentoring.

Talk about the Word more than your wins. Post the verse, not just the quote. Invite a friend into your morning rhythm. Show your children how to fight lies with truth. The world doesn't need more influencers. It requires more warriors of the Word.

Section Wrap-Up: Review & Reflection

What did you DISCOVER about your spirit?

_____

_____

_____

_____

What will you begin to DEVELOP in your spirit?

_____

_____

_____

_____

What will you DEPLOY in your life and your spirit?

_____

_____

_____

_____

What will DUPLICATE and teach someone else about the spirit?

_____

_____

_____

_____

CELEBRATION TIME

You just discovered the power source for your entire life! You've learned that spiritual renewal isn't about perfection—it's about presence. You now understand the Shema (listen with intent to obey), know that "It Is Written" is your weapon against every lie and temptation, and have the blueprint for making your spirit the lead voice in your day. Most importantly, you've discovered that faith comes from hope, and your relationship with God is the foundation that makes everything else possible.

Put this book down and create your first morning altar. Find a quiet place, read one verse out loud, and practice listening to God instead of just hearing words. Call someone and share how you're going to start your day with God's presence before anything else. Thank Him that you don't need to have it all together—you just need to show up. Your spirit is now equipped to lead your mind, soul, and body into complete renewal.

Don't put off being happy for the sake of growing and grinding.

PART 3

THE MIND

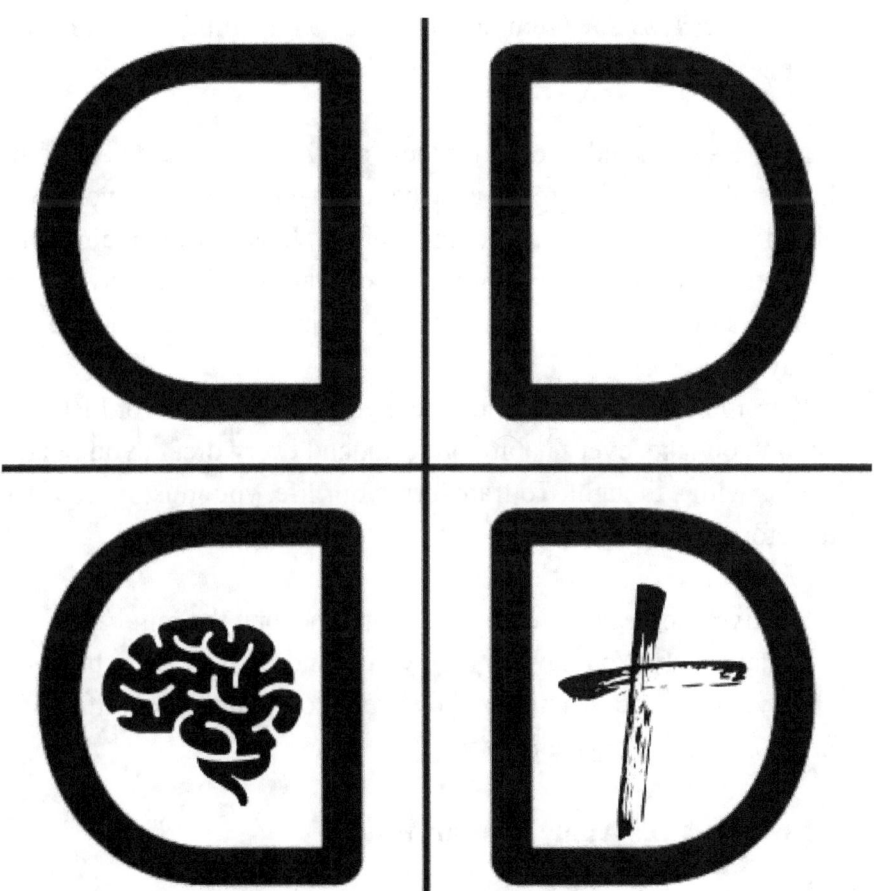

8. MIND: YOU ARE YOUR THOUGHTS

As we discussed in the Discover phase, your identity shapes your reality. **_Proverbs 23:7_** reminds us that as a man thinks in his heart, so is he.

I was 38 years old, mopping floors at 5 AM, when the lies hit me hardest: 'You're a failure. Look where you ended up. Everyone else is ahead of you.' But then something shifted. Instead of agreeing with those thoughts, I started fighting back: 'Wait. Is this actually true? Or is this just fear talking?' That was the beginning of winning the war in my mind.

Your mind is the battlefield where your future is won or lost. Every action you take, every habit you form, and every dream you pursue begins with a thought. To transform your life, you must first transform your thinking.

Positive and negative emotions cannot occupy the mind simultaneously. You have to own your mindset. Own your habits. Own your routine. Anything above zero compounds, so a little effort in the beginning goes a long way.

How the 4 D's Apply to Your Mind:

DISCOVER: The lies you've believed about yourself and identify destructive thought patterns

DEVELOP: New mental habits rooted in God's truth and biblical thinking

DEPLOY: Mental resilience and Renew4D thinking in daily challenges and decisions

DUPLICATE: Teaching others how to win their own mental battles and think biblically

Why Your Mind Matters for Renewal:

Romans 12:2 tells us to "be transformed by the renewing of your mind" because your thoughts determine your actions, your actions create your habits, and your habits shape your destiny. Your mind is either your greatest asset or your biggest obstacle—there's no neutral ground.

What You'll Accomplish:

By the end of this section, you'll know how to identify and replace lies with biblical truth, develop unshakeable mental resilience, and create thought patterns that align with God's plan for your life. You'll move from mental defeat to mental victory.

Your transformation starts with a single thought. Let's make sure it's the right one.

Your mind is a powerful tool, capable of being used for good or for bad. It is a powerful weapon. It can lead you to great heights and achievements. It can also lead you into despair and ruin. It is not always a safe place. The enemy doesn't play fair either. The enemy used every strategy possible to lie and deceive and get you to THINK differently than how God sees you.

My pastor now says something that has always stuck with me. He says, "God doesn't meet you where you pretend to be. He meets you where you ARE." Don't lie to yourself, because God certainly isn't fooled. Take a deep self-introspection, get honest with yourself and God, and go from there.

The war in my mind has been a constant battle since I was young.

My story was always this...

I grew up poor. We didn't vacation at Disneyland or Six Flags. I didn't wear designer clothes. I didn't get to buy a starter jacket or class ring. I didn't have my own car. Our house literally had a mobile dishwasher that you had to wheel up to the sink and attach a hose to the faucet.

The first house I remember, my room was a plywood makeshift bed in the laundry room between the kitchen and the outside back patio. Our second house, my dad built a wall in our second living room to make a room. A) A second living room makes it sound like we had a huge house. We did not. B) No closet in that "room", and now that I think of it, it didn't even have molding around the door so you could peek through the open gap of the shims. All my other friends' parents made more money. Had more things. Life was "easier" for them.

But that's not the whole truth. That's a skewed fragment of the truth. Was everything I just said factual? Yes. But was it reality? Not entirely.

I didn't own Mickey Mouse ears, but I do have a myriad of memories from the sand hill at the beach in Garabldi, Oregon. We would camp there in the summer. That was our big family vacation. Sleeping in a tent on the beach. And, it was terrific.

I didn't have my own car, but I did have my parents' trust to drive their beautiful maroon Chevy Corsica pretty much anywhere I wanted, anytime.

Our house was clean. Our dishes were clean. I was taught the value of responsibility at a young age. I was taught to work for my money. If you want a nice shirt for picture day, save up. I didn't have Abercrombie & Fitch, but I had the lesser Structure clothes. (Child of the 90s).

If I outgrew a space, my dad would literally build a new room for me. My parents never fought. I never saw my dad drunk or yelling.

We were poor in terms of our wallet, but rich in love and work ethic. Little did I know then that those life lessons would be more impactful than growing up with a silver spoon in my mouth.

But it took me years to figure this out. In my early career, I did everything I could to climb the ladder. Success was my focus and only goal. I needed Manager in my title. Then the Director title. Being someone meant having a title and "success" and money and things. It was all a lie. It was all deception. It was a lie.

Craig Groeschel wrote a life-changing book called Winning the War in Your Mind, which builds on the spiritual foundation established in Part 2 and will flow into the habit formation explored in the Soul section. He taught you how to hone in on a lie, tear it down, and replace it with truth. Your life moves in the direction of your strongest thoughts. If those thoughts are lies, you'll find yourself living out their destruction. To change your life, you must change your thinking. You must renew your mind, not just your behaviors.

He doesn't just tell you to *THINK* positive. He gives you a playbook on how to *BE* positive:

- Identify the lies
- Replace them with truth
- Rewire your brain around new pathways
- Reframe your outlook
- Rejoice in spiritual practices

In my life, the lie was that I needed a title and things to prove to people I was successful. The lie was ultimately keeping me from what God had called me to do. I had gifts and callings, dreams and ambitions, that were being pushed down for the sake of "succeeding in life". I wasn't being the person I knew I was.

The bigger truth is this. I had a poverty mindset. A poverty mindset isn't just about money; it's about fear, scarcity, and a distorted sense of identity. I was afraid of not having money. I was afraid of not being able to support my wife, kids, and family. I was afraid that if people didn't think I was valuable in the workplace, I wouldn't be valuable in their personal lives. Aka...I had no true self-confidence.

"If you are broke, you are fighting for survival. If you are going to break through, you are fighting for someone else."

- Sahil Bloom

Find something or someone to fight for that is greater than yourself. The truth is, you'll never really achieve the level of success and potential that is inside of you, unless you look beyond for something greater, to inspire you to do everything it takes, to sacrifice it all, to get there. True breakthrough comes when you shift from survival to service. Fight for something greater than yourself.

Surround yourself with good company. You are what you eat, listen to, and watch. You are who you **believe** you are. Equally, who you hang out with is who your future self will be. Show me your 2-3 closest friends, and I'll show you who you'll be in 5-10 years. Wise counsel and a biblical community are of the utmost importance because they help you maintain a clear mind. Find people to fight for you, and fight with you.

You are not alone in this battle. As you begin to renew your mind, teach others how to win their own mind wars by showing them how you rewrote your inner narrative with God's truth. Model mental resilience fueled by the Spirit. Duplicate your Renew4D mind into others.

A reminder from above...

"Whether you think you can, or you think you can't...you're right."

-    Henry Ford

If you believe you are a nobody, you'll be a nobody. If you think your life sucks and are miserable and a failure, guess what? You are, and will be. You can listen to Tony Robbins or Simon Sinek all day long, but until you renew your mind and start doing, you'll never change. If you stay in your head, you'll never grow.

Remember Pigpen from the Charlie Brown cartoons? All he needed to do was take a bath. One small action could have completely changed his life and altered how others viewed him. But he didn't. He stayed in his filth (literally).

Don't be a pigpen. Be a Hungry Caterpillar. The Hungry Caterpillar ate and ate and ate until he got sick and fat. He didn't wallow in his self-pity. He ate some leafy greens and felt better. Then he accepted his fatness and changed. He transformed into something beautiful.

Maybe you're reading this and thinking, "That sounds like me." If so, you're not alone. The first step to changing our mindset is getting honest about what's actually running through our heads. Let's do a quick audit.

The Mindset Audit

Take a moment to identify the top 3 recurring thoughts that dominate your mind. Are they empowering or destructive?

- "I'll never be healthy enough..."
- "I'm too late to start..."
- "I'm always the one who screws things up..."

Now rewrite them through the lens of biblical truth:

- "God is restoring my health and strength daily."
- "God's timing is perfect—today is not too late."
- "I may have failed before, but I am not a failure."

You cannot transform what you won't identify. This is the start of your mental renovation.

Daily Declarations

Now that we've audited your mindset, I'd like to present a challenge to you. Daily declarations may sound funny at first. But they work. As we learned earlier, this isn't "fake it until you make it." Writing your own daily declaration is a powerful tool for overcoming the lies in your mind.

A daily declaration is simple. You think of an area in your life that you know isn't a representation of what God says it should be. Areas of fear or lack, pain, or anguish. Using what you just learned about changing your paradigm, you will write down a daily declaration that you should speak over your life **daily**.

This is something I've been speaking over my life for years. I've seen a breakthrough. I've seen heartache. Currently, I'm in the lack phase, but I'm still contending for the promises of God and His truth.

Jessee's Financial Declaration

"I live not according to the world and its standards, but in a kingdom economy, and I am a child of God. Destined for victory and to be an overcomer. I am the head and not the tail, the lender and investor and not the borrower. I am blessed to be a blessing, and I will have an abundance for every good work. In Jesus' name!"

See how that completely changed my view of my financial

circumstances? It doesn't sweep anything under the carpet or overlook clear faults or issues. However, it speaks truth into a situation from God's perspective.

"Death and life are in the power of the tongue, and those who love it will eat its fruit."

- Proverbs 18:21

I'm going to take you through a simple exercise to pinpoint and declare a daily declaration in your life. Get your pen and bible ready.

Daily Declaration Challenge

Step 1: Identify the Lie - What area of your life feels stuck, defeated, or contrary to God's promises? Write it down honestly:

The areas I struggle with most:

_____

_____

_____

_____

The lies I've been believing about this area:

_____

_____

_____

_____

Step 2: Find God's Truth - What does Scripture say about this area of your life? Look up verses that counter the lie you've identified:

Biblical truths about my situation:

1. _____

2. _____

3. _____

4. _____

Key verses to remember:

1. _____

2. _____

3. _____

4. _____

Step 3: Write Your Declaration - Now craft your personal daily declaration. Make it present tense, faith-filled, and rooted in God's Word:

My Daily Declaration:

_____

_____

_____

_____

_____

(End with "In Jesus' name!" to seal it with His authority)

Remember: This Isn't Wishful Thinking

Your daily declaration isn't about pretending everything is perfect. It's about aligning your thoughts with God's truth and speaking His promises over the areas where you need a breakthrough. Some days you'll feel it, some days you won't. Speak it anyway. Your feelings will catch up to your faith.

Renew4D Reflection: Win the War in Your Mind

Discover the lie you've believed.

You believed your worth was tied to what you had or what title you held. That growing up without money meant you had less value. That success would silence insecurity. But that was never the whole story.
The real lie? That your identity had to be earned.
The truth? You've always had value because God has given it to you.

Develop truth statements rooted in God's Word.

- "As a man thinks in his heart, so is he." (Proverbs 23:7)
- "I am not conformed to this world, but transformed by the renewing of my mind." (Romans 12:2)

Deploy daily habits that strengthen mental and spiritual resilience.

Start by recognizing the negative mental loops. Then replace them with God's truth every day. Speak truth over your life. Journal your God-given wins. Start each morning with affirmations rooted in Scripture. Keep your environment clean. What you read, watch, listen to, and who you surround yourself with.

Habit Tip: Post your new truth statements on your bathroom mirror. Preach to yourself while you brush your teeth.

Duplicate this mindset shift in others by modeling and mentoring.

Share your mental battle. Don't just talk about the caterpillar—be the butterfly. Show others that true transformation happens from within. Encourage your friends, kids, and coworkers to call out the lies they've believed and replace them with truth. Mentor someone stuck in a scarcity mindset and model abundance through Christ.

9. A MIND RENEW4D

Romans 12:2 says, "Do not be *conformed* to this world, but be *transformed* by the *renewing* of your mind."

Let's get scientific for a moment. Or at least try to sound like it.

Neuroplasticity is the brain's ability to reorganize itself by forming new neural connections throughout life. It enables the brain to adapt in response to learning, experience, injury, or environmental changes.
    Your brain can rewire itself based on what you repeat (habits)—which we'll explore in the Soul section—focus on (God, the spirit), and what you believe or trust (mind). Or as *Proverbs 3:5-6* says, "Trust in the Lord with all your heart, And lean not on your own understanding; In all your ways acknowledge Him, And He shall direct your paths."
    It's not "self-help". It is a biblical transformation backed by brain science. Your brain's ability isn't stuck; it's adaptable, changeable, and wired for renewal. It's science.

Your Brain's Three Pathways to Change

God designed your brain with remarkable flexibility, but not all change happens the same way. Scientists have identified three types of neuroplasticity: your brain's ability to rewire itself:

Passive plasticity occurs naturally, especially in childhood, when your brain absorbs information like a sponge. This is why children learn languages effortlessly while adults struggle. Your brain was most moldable then, but it's not stuck now.

Maladaptive plasticity happens when trauma or negative experiences create destructive neural pathways. Think of it as your brain learning survival patterns that once protected you but now hold you back. Those lies you believed about yourself? They carved deep grooves in your thinking through repetition and emotional intensity.

Adaptive plasticity is your secret weapon. It's the type you can *actively* cultivate at any age. This is where biblical mind renewal meets brain science. To harness adaptive plasticity, you must engage in deliberate practice, step outside your comfort zone, and embrace mistakes as opportunities for your brain to evolve.

One tool that really helped me during this rewiring season was the Pause app by John Eldredge. He wrote a book shortly after COVID called Resilience. It's a great book, inspiring, and super beneficial to my life during this season of transformation. However, the Pause app offers 1-, 3-, 5-, or more-minute "pauses" that feature soft worship music in the background while John or his wife guides you through a brief time of pause and devotion. It's a great time just to sit and be quiet. Listen. Hear what God is saying.

This app is also beneficial in those days when you're barely meeting your C-Goal. When the world is against you, you're frustrated, angry, sad, and depressed. This app helps calm your spirit and mind, allowing you to be in His presence. I highly recommend this app and tool in your life.

Just like your diet shapes your physical health, your mental health is shaped by what you consume daily. What are you watching? Who are you listening to? What content is filling your scroll time?

Philippians 4:8 says, "to think on things that are true, noble, right, pure, lovely, admirable, excellent, and praiseworthy." Are your inputs matching that filter?

If not, it's time to do a mental detox. Clear out the noise. Create more space for God's voice. Take a pause.

I lead a men's group at my church, and we have an ongoing joke about my co-leader and me having stock in the Pause app. Every time we mention it, we receive a check in the mail. I wish. But we use it. We share it. We've seen the benefit of just stopping and pausing in so many men in our group. It takes a Renew4D mindset to even consider stopping during a busy, chaotic day. It takes a special type of spiritual peace and inner fortitude to walk away from all the noise, in the moment, and be quiet. Pausing is your defense...yet, it is also an offensive tool. Because, although it blocks out the noise, you come away feeling filled and walking in power.

The Celebration Secret: Small Wins, Big Changes

Here's where most people get transformation wrong: they wait until the end to celebrate. But your brain needs dopamine, the neurotransmitter associated with pleasure and motivation, throughout the journey, not just at the destination.

By celebrating small victories, you trigger the release of dopamine, making the renewal process more enjoyable and sustainable. This means setting action-based goals and rewarding the process, not just the outcome. Celebrate when you speak your daily declaration, not when your circumstances change. Reward yourself when you replace one negative thought with God's truth, not when you feel completely transformed.

This approach keeps you motivated and in love with the renewal process. But here's the key: keep varying your rewards to maintain that dopamine rush. Your brain adapts quickly, so what excited you last week may feel routine this week. Mix up your celebrations. Sometimes it's a favorite coffee, sometimes it's calling a friend to share your victory, sometimes it's simply pausing to thank God for the progress.

Remember, every small win is rewiring your brain toward the person God created you to be. You're not just changing your thoughts, you're literally reshaping your neural pathways through the power of celebration and biblical truth. Those small victories and taking time to enjoy them and have some fun, rewires and changes your adaptive plasticity.

God gave you the power to rewire your brain. Science calls it neuroplasticity. Scripture calls it renewing your mind. You can tear down lies by replacing them with God's Word—truth is your weapon.

Every battle you fight externally was first won or lost in your mind. Thoughts are not just passing ideas—they are spiritual weapons or spiritual strongholds. What lies have you accepted as truth? What thoughts are driving your decisions?

When challenges come, your thoughts decide your response. Reframe the situation. Instead of "This is too hard," say, "God is with me, and I'm equipped." Instead of "I'm stuck," say, "This is my setup for growth."

That same day in October 2022 marked the beginning of my mental transformation. It was that word from the Lord that catapulted me into my future. It was not overnight, though I wish it were. As I write this, it has been almost five years since that morning. But my mindset now, compared to 2020, is vastly different. It's been rewired. It's been Renew4D.

Towards the end of 2024, I yet again found myself in a spot of complacency, apathy, and hopelessness. I had gained weight...again. Gotten lazy...again. I just lost track of all that the Lord had done and showed me, and like Peter, I was sinking in the water when I lost sight of the ultimate price.

However, I yet again found renewal. I made a declaration to myself and to God that 2025 would be a different year. It would be a year of stepping out. A year of action. A year of hard work. A year of uncomfortability.

I needed a change; body, soul, mind, and spirit. Using the Four D's, I began with my spirit, as you learned in the last few chapters. Then came my mind. This was step 2, the second phase in my life's renewal.

It wasn't just a New Year's resolution. It was a life commitment. It began in and with my spirit. Then, if I had any hope of really achieving what God had in store for me, my mind needed to follow. I stopped talking badly about my health and my weight. I made changes to my diet. In the final section of this book, we'll go over the body and what I did to bring victory to that area of my life.

I stopped thinking and started writing things down. I stopped Googling and asking ChatGPT for advice, and began meeting with real people, getting accountability, and taking practical steps to achieve the dreams and visions that were coming back to me. I stopped making Amazon wish lists and started investing in myself.

In six short months, my life was completely changed. The most significant change, though, was the literal renewal of my mind. I stopped all anti-depression medication in June of 2025. My mind was Renew4D, and I felt amazing. The balanced diet and nutrition helped a lot, but thinking differently is what changed my life. I wasn't reliant on medication anymore because my mind was restored and back to thinking positively, powerfully, and with purpose.

Now I'm not recommending you come off your medication. Please understand that. (And for legal reasons, I am not recommending it.) BUT..again, that's a big but...if you truly renew your mind as the Bible says you can, you are 100% capable of living a med-free life! I promise if you make conscious decisions to rewire your brain, start speaking and living more truth, think about yourself differently, and begin to act, you'll feel greater than you have in your entire life.

"The biggest wall you have to climb is the one you build in your mind... To get your mind on the right track, the rest will follow."

- Roy T. Bennett

This all goes back to identity. If you begin to realize your true identity, your mind will follow. You can't help but live Renew4D if you are walking in your God-given identity. Living in the lies and defeat is ultimately just living without identity and purpose.

I haven't done this yet, but I'd like to end this section with a prayer. Feel free to join with me, and repeat as you read.

"Lord, I give you my thoughts. Every fearful one, every shame-filled one, every lie that has taken root. Uproot the things that aren't from You. Plant your truth deep in me. Renew my mind so I can live in the freedom, power, and purpose You've called me to. I believe You are not finished with me. I am being transformed by the renewing of my mind, starting today. Amen."

You've just begun the most important mental shift of your life. Don't stop here. Don't wait for perfection. Start where you are, with what you have, and let your Renew4D mind lead the way. The thoughts you think today are building the future you'll live tomorrow. Let's build something worthy of the call God has placed on your life.

🧠 Renew4D Reflection: Renewing Your Mind

Discover the lie you've believed.

You believed your thoughts were permanent. That anxiety, defeat, and apathy were just part of who you are. That your brain couldn't change. That you'd never break free from cycles of laziness, fear, or failure. But here's the truth: you are not stuck. God designed your mind to be rewired.

Develop truth statements rooted in God's Word.

- "Do not be conformed to this world, but be transformed by the renewing of your mind." (Romans 12:2)
- "Trust in the Lord with all your heart... and He shall direct your paths." (Proverbs 3:5-6)
- "You have the mind of Christ." (1 Corinthians 2:16)
- "As a man thinks in his heart, so is he." (Proverbs 23:7)

Deploy daily habits that strengthen mental and spiritual resilience.

Start by identifying the lie, then counter it with Scripture. Rewire your thought patterns by writing them down, speaking truth over your life, and eliminating the noise that leads to doubt. Feed your brain better inputs:
- Less scrolling, more Scripture
- Less wishing, more writing
- Less Googling, more accountability
- Less negativity, more nutrition (mental and physical)

🔧 Habit Tip:

Build a 10-minute "Mind Reset" routine every morning:

1. Read one verse about your identity
2. Write one truth statement
3. Repeat one declaration out loud

Duplicate this mindset shift in others by modeling and mentoring.

Don't just talk about transformation—live it out. Share your before-and-after mindset story. Help others walk through their own mental rewiring. Show them that it's not just possible. It's God's will for their life. Invite them into the process. Be real. Be raw. Be Renew4D.

Section Wrap-Up: Review & Reflection

What did you DISCOVER about your mind?

_____

_____

_____

_____

What will you begin to DEVELOP in your mind?

_____

_____

_____

_____

What will you DEPLOY in your life and your mind?

_____

_____

_____

_____

What will DUPLICATE and teach someone else about the mind?

_____

_____

_____

_____

CELEBRATION TIME

You just conquered the battlefield of your mind! You've discovered that your thoughts aren't permanent, learned how to identify lies and replace them with God's truth, and understood that your brain is literally designed to be rewired through neuroplasticity. You now have daily declarations, the power to celebrate small wins for dopamine rewards, and a complete system for mental renewal. Most importantly, you've realized that your identity in Christ is the foundation for every thought pattern you build.

Put this book down and go celebrate this mental breakthrough. Write your first daily declaration and speak it out loud. Call someone and share how you're going to rewire one specific lie you've been believing. Take a victory walk and thank God that your mind can be transformed through His truth, not just positive thinking. Your mental resilience is about to change everything—and that deserves a celebration right now.

Don't put off being happy for the sake of growing and grinding.

PART 4

THE SOUL

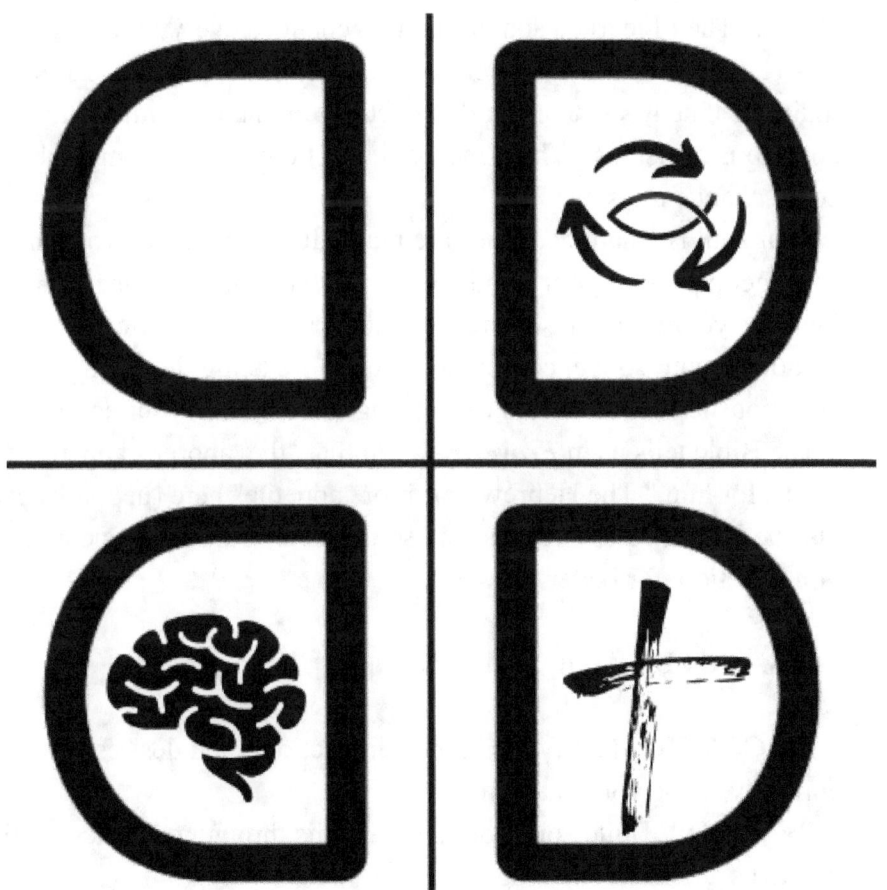

10. I'M A SOUL MAN

I used to think I was just 'not a morning person.' Every day started with hitting the snooze button, grabbing coffee, and feeling behind before I even began. My soul felt chaotic because my habits were chaotic. Then I learned something that changed everything: my soul wasn't the problem. My systems were. Duke University research indicates that 40-80% of our daily actions are habits, rather than conscious decisions. Which means that if I could change my habits, I could change my soul.

Your soul is where decisions are made. It's the realm of your inner life, encompassing your mind, heart, will, and imagination. Your soul includes your thoughts, desires, passions, and dreams. More than just emotions, your soul encompasses your entire being, including consciousness, desires, and the driving force behind your actions.

The Bible tells us in **Proverbs 16:26** that "the laborer's appetite works for him." The Hebrew word for "appetite" here (nephesh) can also be translated as "desires" or "soul." Your soul's desires compel you to action, for better or worse.

How the 4 D's Apply to Your Soul:

DISCOVER: Identify the habits, distractions, and desires that currently shape your character

DEVELOP: Build soul-nourishing habits through consistent daily practices and habit stacking

DEPLOY: Live out your transformed character in relationships and daily decisions

DUPLICATE: Model healthy soul habits and mentor others in character development

Why Your Soul Matters for Renewal:

Your habits shape your soul, and your habits determine your destiny. Whether positive or negative, habits significantly impact your soul by shaping your inner state, influencing your relationships, and ultimately affecting your overall well-being and sense of purpose.

Positive habits nurture inner peace, strengthen relationships, promote purpose and meaning, and enhance overall well-being. Negative habits cause inner disquiet, damage relationships, diminish meaning and purpose, and hinder your growth and potential.

What You'll Accomplish:

By the end of this section, you'll understand how to identify soul-damaging habits, replace them with soul-nourishing practices, and create a rhythm of small daily improvements that yield huge results over time. You'll learn that faithfulness with small things leads to excellence in big things.

Habits, whether positive or negative, significantly impact your well-being by shaping your inner state, influencing your relationships, and ultimately affecting your overall sense of purpose.

Here's a more detailed look:

Positive Habits:

- Nurture Inner Peace: Practices like gratitude, mindfulness, and spending time in nature can cultivate a sense of calm and contentment.
- Strengthen Relationships: Acts of kindness, compassion, and active listening can foster deeper connections with others and

enhance your ability to connect with your own inner self.

- Promote Purpose and Meaning: Engaging in activities that align with your values, helping others, or pursuing your passions can lead to a greater sense of purpose and fulfillment.
- Enhance Overall Well-being: Healthy habits, such as regular exercise, sufficient sleep, and a balanced diet, contribute to both physical and mental well-being, which in turn positively impact your overall well-being.

Negative Habits:

- Cause Inner Disquiet: Habits like negativity, self-criticism, and procrastination can lead to feelings of anxiety, stress, and dissatisfaction.
- Damage Relationships: Unhealthy habits, such as gossiping, manipulation, or emotional outbursts, can damage relationships and create distance between individuals.
- Diminish Meaning and Purpose: Focusing on superficial things or avoiding challenges can lead to a sense of emptiness and a lack of purpose.
- Hinder Growth and Potential: Neglecting negative habits can limit your potential and prevent you from reaching your full potential.

Examples of Soul-Nourishing Habits:

- Gratitude: Regularly expressing thanks for the good things in your life can shift your focus towards positivity.
- Mindfulness: Paying attention to the present moment can help you appreciate the beauty and richness of life.
- Spending Time in nature can be a source of inspiration and renewal, as it allows us to connect with the natural world.
- Helping Others: Acts of service and compassion can bring a

sense of meaning and purpose.

- Self-Compassion: Treating yourself with kindness and understanding, especially during challenging times, is essential for maintaining emotional well-being.

Examples of Soul-Damaging Habits:

- Negativity: Focusing on the negative aspects of life can lead to a pessimistic outlook and a lack of joy.
- Self-Criticism: Constant self-doubt and criticism can erode your self-esteem and sense of worth.
- Procrastination: Putting things off can lead to stress, anxiety, and a sense of being overwhelmed.
- Excessive Materialism: Fixating on possessions can lead to a lack of contentment and a preoccupation with external validation.
- Lack of Self-Care: Neglecting your physical and mental health can lead to burnout and a decline in overall well-being

Your habits are the architects of your soul. Every daily choice either builds you up or tears you down, shaping your inner peace, relationships, and sense of purpose. Soul-nourishing habits, such as gratitude, mindfulness, acts of service, and self-compassion, create a foundation of contentment and meaningful connections. In contrast, soul-damaging habits like negativity, self-criticism, procrastination, and excessive materialism breed anxiety, damaged relationships, and emptiness.

The power lies in recognizing that small, consistent improvements compound over time—faithfulness in little things creates excellence in big things. By intentionally replacing destructive patterns with life-giving practices, you not only change what you do, but you also transform who you become.

"If you are going to achieve excellence in big things, you develop the habit in little matters."

- Colin Powell

Your soul is built one habit at a time, so let's make sure they're the right ones. Your soul operates on rhythm. The steady beat of daily habits that either build you up or tear you down. Think of habit formation like a piñata: invisible progress is accumulated with every hit it takes. You can't see the internal damage until suddenly, with one final swing, everything breaks open and the reward spills out.

That's the power of consistent, small actions. As research shows us, "Small, daily, seemingly insignificant improvements, when done consistently over time, yield staggering results." This is "faithfulness with the small things" that we learned about earlier.

The key is to focus on these micro-actions, rather than striving for perfection. After all, perfectionism often hinders progress.

The Soul's Three Key Questions:

So how do you actually audit and improve your soul habits? I learned a simple framework from Rob Dial that cuts through the complexity and gets straight to what matters.

Rob Dial challenges us to regularly ask: "What should I start, stop, and continue doing to stay on course?" These three questions, when applied to your soul, become:

START: What soul-nourishing habits will you begin? (Gratitude, mindfulness, acts of service)

STOP: What soul-damaging habits will you eliminate? (Negativity, self-criticism, excessive materialism)

CONTINUE: What positive patterns are already working that you need to maintain?

Take Back Your Time

Most people spend 1-4 hours daily on social media and TV. If you can reclaim just one of those hours, that's 30 hours a month. A full day, you get back to investing in your soul's development. The question isn't whether you have time; it's whether you'll choose to use it wisely.

Your soul is where your decisions are made. It's the realm of your mind, will, and emotions that shapes your character. As **Proverbs 16:26** tells us, "the desires of your soul compel you to action (habits)." Let's ensure those actions are shaped by habits worthy of your calling in Christ.

Though he's an evil tyrant, Thanos most eloquently states, "The hardest choices require the strongest wills." Are you willing to create new habits that may seem boring or inconsequential, in order to see your life fully Renew4D? Or will you snub your nose at the sacrifices needed to achieve that, and live a life of mediocrity and right at average, if not slightly under?

Craig Groeschel, in his book The Power to Change, emphasizes that lasting transformation happens through small, consistent changes rather than dramatic overhauls. This aligns perfectly with what we see in Scripture and science. Your soul is shaped by the rhythm of daily decisions, not momentary bursts of motivation.

His approach perfectly complements our 4 D's framework. You Discover God's design for your life, Develop small habits aligned with that design, Deploy those habits consistently in your daily routine, and Duplicate the transformation by helping others change as well.

Think of a piñata. You are blindfolded when trying to hit it. You aren't quite sure where it is, and even worse, it's on the move. But you know what's inside it. You know what the reward is. With each grazing hit, the piñata weakens. Eventually, after enough willpower, stamina, determination, and strength...BOOM...the piñata busts open and the rewards are yours for the taking. The piñata is your ultimate goal, your reason for doing this. Your habits are each swing you take. The results...after enough habitual swings, you'll hit the target enough to get the prize.

So again, I ask you. What could you do with 30 hours a month? Think of the books you could read, the podcasts you could listen to, the protein shakes you could make, and the miles you could walk.

Your soul transformation isn't about willpower; it's about habit power. Every small daily choice is either building the person God designed you to be or tearing down your potential. The 30 hours you could reclaim each month, the micro-actions you take consistently, and the rhythm you establish today will determine who you become tomorrow. Craig Groeschel reminds us that lasting change occurs through small, consistent steps aligned with God's design for our lives. Your habits are the architects of your soul, and with the 4 D's framework, you now have the blueprint to build well.

The question isn't whether soul transformation is possible. It's whether you're willing to start. Right now, today, with the very next decision you make.

Will you **START** one soul-nourishing habit this week?

Will you **STOP** one soul-damaging pattern that's been holding you back?

Will you **CONTINUE** building on the positive rhythms already working in your life?

Your piñata moment is coming. Every small swing, every moment of gratitude, every act of service, every time you choose truth over negativity, is weakening the barriers between you and the life God has planned. You can't see the progress happening inside, but it's accumulating. The breakthrough is closer than you think.

Renew4D Reflection: Habits Shape Your Soul

Discover the lie you've believed.

You may have believed your soul was simply emotional. Those feelings were fleeting and irrelevant, or worse, unchangeable. But the truth is, your soul is where your decisions are made. It's the engine room of your desires, character, and will. And it's being shaped—every day—by your habits. Every small choice helps sculpt your identity and destiny.

Develop truth statements rooted in God's Word.

- "The laborer's appetite works for him; his hunger drives him on." – Proverbs 16:26 (appetite = nephesh = soul)
- "What good will it be for someone to gain the whole world, yet forfeit their soul?" – Matthew 16:26
- "Above all else, guard your heart, for everything you do flows from it." – Proverbs 4:23
- "If you are going to achieve excellence in big things, you develop the habit in little matters." – Colin Powell

Your soul is formed in the mundane, in the small and faithful, not in the occasional high of spiritual hype.

Deploy daily habits that strengthen your soul.

Your soul thrives in rhythm. Like a drumbeat, the small daily habits that seem insignificant are doing eternal work. Start here:

- Practice gratitude every morning.
- Say no to comparison and criticism.
- Spend a few quiet minutes in stillness or prayer before the noise of the day begins.

105

- Help someone without recognition.
- Reclaim 1 hour a day from scrolling and give it to soul-building instead.

⚒ **Habit Tip:** Use the "Start, Stop, Continue" check-in weekly.

- **START** a soul-nourishing habit: journaling, solitude, gratitude, serving.
- **STOP** a soul-damaging habit: negativity, procrastination, gossip, self-criticism.
- **CONTINUE** the habits that are already producing fruit in your life.

You don't need willpower. You need **habit power.** And Duke University research says up to 80% of our daily life is shaped by these unconscious routines.

Duplicate this mindset shift in others by modeling and mentoring.

Model soulful living. Don't just talk about peace, embody it. Show your spouse, your kids, your friends how to build their soul through consistency.

Mentor someone younger in the faith. Invite a friend to join you in a journaling or gratitude habit for 30 days. Give away a copy of this book or a journal as a tool.

Remember: your transformation is the blueprint for someone else's breakthrough.

11. CREATE A PAST THAT HAS A FUTURE

I once heard a man say, "Who you are today, is who you are tomorrow." There is truth to that. Ultimately, who you are today is the same person you are going to be tomorrow, UNLESS you start changing yourself today, to be the man/woman of God that you desire to be tomorrow. Or, less confusing: If you want to be someone, such as a person of integrity, morals, strong beliefs, and convictions, you will never reach that full potential in Christ unless you make the necessary changes in your life today.

A drug addict can never truly change his ways unless he admits he has a problem and makes steps towards overcoming it. God can do whatever He wants to whomever He wants to. I'm not invalidating God's power. But we have the decision to change our lives.

Why do most New Year's resolutions fail? "I'm gonna lose 20 pounds," but the person can't stop sneaking Sonic blasts (guilty). I'm gonna start my diet tomorrow. However, it often gets pushed back to next week, or next month, or the resolution for the following year. "I'm gonna get my finances in order," but you can't stop charging things to your credit card (guilty). They never really put their foot down or made a change.

Unless we make practical steps to overcome our issues, we will never reach our full potential and growth in Christ. Therefore, since we can't change the past, and tomorrow will soon be in the past, we need to "create a past that has a future!" Think about that. Everything you do right now, in the moment, instantaneously becomes the past.

Who you want to be tomorrow, you should act like that today. What you tolerate, you will become. What you don't stand up for is what you'll allow others to do to you. We've all heard these expressions. But who really does something about it? I desire to be a man of integrity and character, a man of discipline and strong beliefs that won't blow with the wind. I want to live a conviction-filled life, where the spirit of God and my convictions lead me wholeheartedly.

Habit Stacking

How am I going to accomplish who I want to be? That is where Habit Stacking comes in. Habit stacking is the practice of connecting a new habit you want to develop to an existing habit you already do consistently. Instead of trying to find completely new time in your schedule, you "stack" the new behavior onto something you're already doing automatically.

Why Habit Stacking Works

1. Leverages Existing Neural Pathways
Your brain has already formed strong neural pathways for habits you consistently engage in. When you attach a new habit to an established one, you're borrowing that existing "mental highway" instead of building a completely new road.

2. Eliminates Decision Fatigue
You don't have to remember to do the new habit because it's automatically triggered by something you already do. The existing habit becomes your cue.

3. Creates Natural Flow
Instead of forcing new habits into random times, you create logical sequences that feel natural and sustainable.

Examples of Habit Stacking

Soul/Spiritual Habits:

"After I pour my morning coffee, I will read one Bible verse."

"After I brush my teeth at night, I will write three things I'm grateful for."

"After I sit down at my desk, I will pray for 2 minutes."

"After I put my kids to bed, I will spend 5 minutes in quiet reflection."

Mind/Mental Habits:

"After I check my morning alarm, I will speak one positive affirmation."

"After I sit in my car, I will listen to an educational podcast."

"After I eat lunch, I will read one page of a growth book."

"After I close my laptop for the day, I will journal for 5 minutes."

Body/Physical Habits:

"After I wake up, I will drink a full glass of water."

"After I put on my work clothes, I will do 10 push-ups."

"After I eat dinner, I will take a 10-minute walk."

"After I watch the evening news, I will stretch for 5 minutes."

Relationship/Service Habits:

"After I check my phone in the morning, I will text one person encouragement."

"After I get home from work, I will ask my spouse about their day."

"After I have my morning coffee, I will pray for someone specific."

How to Build Effective Habit Stacks

1. Choose Strong Anchor Habits

Pick existing habits that are:

- **Automatic** (you do them without thinking)
- **Consistent** (you do them at the same time/place)
- **Specific** (clear beginning and end)

Good anchors: Brushing teeth, making coffee, sitting down to eat, checking phone alarm

Poor anchors: "When I have time," "When I feel motivated," "During lunch" (too vague)

2. Start Small

- Begin with 1-2 minute habits maximum
- Focus on consistency over intensity
- You can always expand later once the habit is established

3. Make It Logical

Stack habits in a way that makes sense:

- **Location-based:** "After I sit at my kitchen table, I will read Scripture."
- **Time-based:** "After I turn off my bedroom light, I will pray."
- **Energy-based:** "After I exercise, I will make a protein shake."

4. Be Specific

Vague: "After I wake up, I will pray."

Specific: "After I turn off my bedroom alarm, I will pray for 3 minutes while still in bed."

Common Mistakes to Avoid

1. Starting Too Big
Don't stack "After I brush my teeth, I will exercise for 30 minutes."
Start with "After I brush my teeth, I will do five push-ups."

2. Choosing Weak Anchors
Avoid anchoring to habits you don't do consistently or at random times.

3. Ignoring Context
Don't stack incompatible habits: "After I get in my car, I will meditate for 10 minutes" (Not safe!)

4. Trying to Stack Too Many at Once
Start with ONE habit stack. Master it for 2-4 weeks before adding another.

Remember: You're not trying to become perfect overnight. You're building an architecture of small, consistent actions that compound over time. A daily 2-minute habit stacked onto existing routines becomes 12+ hours of soul development per year.

> *"You do not rise to the level of your goals. You fall to the level of your systems."*

> \-   James Clear

I learned this from James Clear's Atoms habit app. It's a great way to summarize the cycle of habit-forming improvements.

The Cycle of Improvement

1. **Awareness** - Identify what you need to improve.

2. **Deliberate practice** - Focus your conscious effort on the specific area you want to improve.
3. **Habit** - With practice, the effort becomes automatic.
4. **Repeat** - Begin the cycle anew.

Your soul won't transform by accident. It requires intentional daily habits aligned with the 4 D's. Start by discovering through prayer who God designed you to be, and then honestly assess the current habits that shape your character. You already know what needs to change.

Next, develop small, consistent practices that draw your soul closer to Christ-likeness. Remember, faithfulness in small things leads to greater responsibilities.

Then deploy these habits daily, choosing to "die daily" as Paul describes in *1 Corinthians 15:31*, dying to old patterns and living out your Renew4D identity.

Finally, duplicate this soul transformation by mentoring others in character development.

Don't wait for the perfect moment or until you feel completely ready. The soul you desire to have is built through today's choices, not tomorrow's intentions. Jesus is returning, and your character preparation happens one habit at a time. Let your daily practices be acts of worship, shaping your soul for His kingdom purposes.

Napoleon Hill reminds us to "cherish your dreams," but dreams without disciplined habits remain fantasies. Your habits are creating a past that has a future. Every small choice today is writing the story of who you'll become tomorrow.

"The soul has no regrets with good intentions."

-   Anthony Douglass Williams

Good intentions alone aren't enough. The question you must ask yourself is: Are you working the rhythm, or are you worried about the result? If you work within the daily rhythm, creating good habits, your soul and life will have zero regrets. It is impossible to be sad about living a fulfilling life of change and renewal.

Renew4D Reflection: Create a Past That Has a Future

Discover the lie you've believed.

You may have believed your past disqualifies your future. That change is too slow, or that you're "stuck" in who you are today. But here's the truth: every moment you live becomes your past—so why not fill it with decisions you're proud of? You can create a past that supports your future by building it one choice at a time. Every action today becomes tomorrow's testimony.

Develop truth statements and new rhythms.

- "You do not rise to the level of your goals. You fall to the level of your systems." — James Clear
- "Create a past that has a future."
- "I die daily." — 1 Corinthians 15:31
- "The soul has no regrets with good intentions." — Anthony Douglass Williams

You don't need perfection. You need a plan. That plan is built on daily, stacked habits that align with who you want to be.

Deploy habit stacks that shape your soul, mind, body, and relationships.

Start with one simple stack. Build from there. Stack soul habits on top of your coffee. Stack mental growth to your commute. Stack physical movement onto routines like dressing or dinner. Stack kindness and connection after common triggers, such as phone checks or walks through the door.

⟳ Example Habit Stacks:

- After I make coffee, I will write one sentence of gratitude.
- After I brush my teeth, I will stretch for 2 minutes.
- After I sit at my desk, I will pray for someone by name.
- After I check my morning alarm, I will say one truth statement aloud.

🔧 **Habit Tip:** Focus on rhythm, not results.

You're building a system, not chasing a spark of motivation. When you stack habits onto existing anchors, you create consistency. When you keep it small, you keep it sustainable. When you repeat, you reinforce. Your system becomes your story.

Duplicate this transformation in others.

Show others how to turn "good intentions" into lasting integrity. Mentor a student, a friend, or your child in habit stacking. Share your own rhythm of growth, including your journaling and morning routine. Let your systems speak louder than your words. You'll be surprised who starts to copy the quiet patterns of your discipline.

⏳ **Final Challenge:**

This week, don't just dream of a future. Create a past worth looking back on.

Stack one habit.
Track it for 7 days.
Journal how you feel by day 8.

Remember: You're not trying to overhaul your life. You're trying to architect it.

Every new action you take becomes your history.
Every stacked habit becomes your legacy.

And that's how you **create a past that has a future.**

Section Wrap-Up: Review & Reflection

What did you DISCOVER about your soul?

_____

_____

_____

_____

What will you begin to DEVELOP in your soul?

_____

_____

_____

_____

What will you DEPLOY in your life and your soul?

_____

_____

_____

_____

What will DUPLICATE and teach someone else about the soul?

_____

_____

_____

_____

CELEBRATION TIME

You just discovered the blueprint for soul transformation! You didn't just read about habits—you learned that your soul is built one small decision at a time, and you now have the tools to architect the character God designed you to have. You understand habit stacking, how to reclaim 30 hours monthly for soul development, and what it means to "create a past that has a future." That's massive progress worth celebrating right now.

Put this book down and go celebrate. Call someone and share your biggest breakthrough from these chapters. Take a victory walk and thank God for showing you how small, consistent actions compound into soul transformation. Start your first habit stack today. Your excitement about growth is contagious, and when you share what you've learned, you inspire others to pursue their own renewal.

Don't put off being happy for the sake of growing and grinding.

PART 5

THE BODY

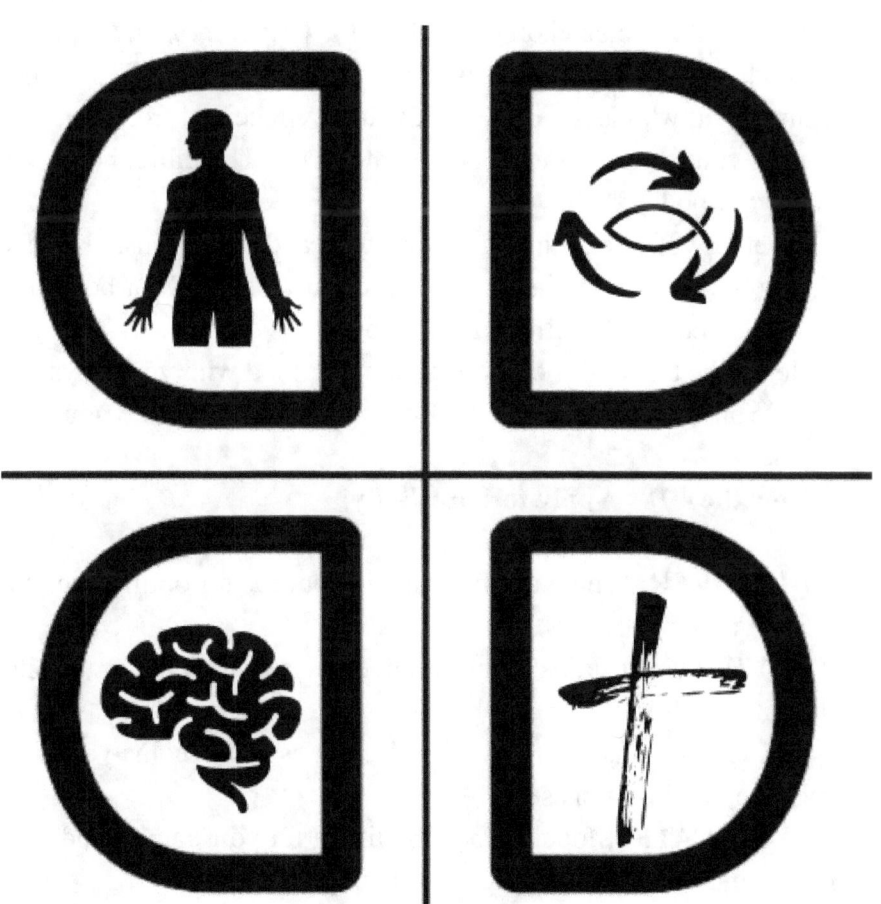

12. MAKING SENSE OF YOUR BODY

Your body is the temple of the Holy Spirit and the vehicle for every calling God has placed on your life. As *1 Corinthians 6:19-20* reminds us, "Do you not know that your bodies are temples of the Holy Spirit, who is in you, whom you have received from God? You are not your own; you were bought at a price. Therefore, honor God with your bodies."

Whether you're dealing with new aches and limitations, or you're young but already feeling the effects of poor habits, your body might not be supporting the life you want to live.

Here's the truth: it's not too late to honor God with your physical temple and condition your body to run the race set before you.

How the 4 D's Apply to Your Body:

DISCOVER: What your body actually needs for optimal health, energy, and longevity

DEVELOP: Sustainable nutrition, exercise, and recovery habits that fit your life

DEPLOY: Consistent physical disciplines that become your lifestyle, not just a phase

DUPLICATE: Modeling healthy living for your family and mentoring others in physical stewardship

Why Your Body Matters for Renewal:
Your body isn't separate from your spiritual life; it's integral to it.

120

When your body is strong and healthy, you have the energy to pursue your calling, the stamina to serve others, and the longevity to see your legacy fulfilled. Physical weakness limits spiritual impact. You can't run the race effectively if your temple is crumbling.

What You'll Accomplish:

By the end of this section, you'll understand how to fuel your body for sustained energy, develop exercise habits that strengthen rather than exhaust you, and create a physical foundation that supports your spiritual, mental, and emotional renewal. You'll move from physical decline to physical stewardship.

Jim Rohn said, "Take care of your body. It's the only place you have to live." But more than that, it's the vessel God chose to house His Spirit and accomplish His purposes through you.

Your physical renewal starts with honoring the temple God gave you.

God intentionally designed every aspect of our physical bodies. He meticulously crafted us in His image. Our senses are gifts to be stewarded, not taken for granted. Physical health affects our ability to worship and serve effectively. Taking care of our bodies honors the Creator who formed them. Our physical experience of the world is meant to point us toward spiritual truth.

Our body has five main senses. The five traditional senses are **sight**, **hearing**, **taste**, **smell**, and **touch**. Each one serves both practical and spiritual purposes in your life.

Physical renewal isn't just about looking good; it's about optimizing the temple God gave you so all your senses can function as He designed them to serve His purposes through your life.

"You are fearfully and wonderfully made."

-    Psalm 139:14

God made you perfect, at least in the beginning. After 40 years, two kids, many jobs, miles, houses moved, trips and falls, back surgeries, and pains, it's less perfect. But it can still be used.

I once saw Kari Jobe at a church, and she designed her entire show around incorporating the senses to worship God and be worshiped by God. Her set was visually beautiful. The sound was obviously angelic. They had meet-and-greets before, so there were other elements to engage the senses.

She explained that, because God created and gave us those senses, we should do everything possible to utilize them.

How They Work Together:

- **Integration**: Your brain combines input from all senses to create your complete experience of reality.
- **Compensation**: When one sense is diminished, others often become more sensitive or stronger.
- **Memory**: Senses trigger powerful memories and emotions.
- **Survival**: All five work together to keep you safe and thriving.

Each sense is a gift from God that affects your physical health and spiritual life. What you see influences your thoughts and desires. What you hear shapes your beliefs and emotions. What you taste affects your nutrition and health. What you smell impacts your environment and mood. What you touch connects you to others and your world.

Your senses are tools for experiencing God's creation and serving His purposes through your physical body.

Each of the senses has a powerful spiritual connection. Each sense can be strengthened, like a muscle. Each sense can be explored further, developed strongly, deployed daily, and even taught so that others can do the same. Every aspect of your life is intertwined, so I'd be remiss to proceed in the Body chapters without discussing quite possibly the most important aspects of the body.

THE 5 SENSES

SIGHT
Navigate environment, recognize faces/objects, read, appreciate beauty

"THE EYE IS THE LAMP OF THE BODY" (MATTHEW 6:22)

TASTE
Food safety, nutrition guidance, pleasure in eating

"TASTE AND SEE THAT THE LORD IS GOOD" (PSALM 34:8)

HEARING
Communication, music appreciation, danger awareness, learning

"FAITH COMES FROM HEARING" (ROMANS 10:17)

SMELL
Food safety, memory triggers, attraction, danger detection

"WE ARE THE AROMA OF CHRIST" (2 CORINTHIANS 2:15)

TOUCH
Physical interaction, safety, comfort, connection with others

"SOMEONE TOUCHED ME; POWER HAS GONE OUT FROM ME" (LUKE 8:46)

Understanding your senses is one thing, but stewarding them intentionally is another. Here are practical ways to honor God through each sense:

SIGHT

Your sight is clearer for reading Scripture and seeing needs around you. When you see clearly, you become more aware of your surroundings. Your peripheral vision also becomes heightened, both spiritually and physically.

On the flipside, as Jesus tells us, the eye is the lamp of the body. What we let in affects who we are, what we do, what we say, and who we become. It directly affects our soul if we are watching things we shouldn't be watching on our phone, or physical or derogatory movies. We need to guard our hearts, but more importantly, our eyes.

Be mindful of what we let in through our eye gates.

Sight Habits to Build

- Scripture before screens.
- Adult content locks on screens and phones.
- Go outside and get 15 minutes of sunlight every morning.
- Limit blue light (from phones and TVs) before bedtime.
- Digital sabbath one day a week

TASTE

Your taste guides you toward proper nutrition. Your tongue can be something to be experienced. New cuisines, cultures, and ethnicities all at your tastebuds. But taste directly affects your weight. Let's be honest. I LOVE food. I love ice cream. I love pizza. I love a lot of stuff that isn't good for my body. This is probably the hardest area in my personal life, which is cutting out sweets and fast food. Why? Because it all tastes SOOOOOOOO good.

Taste Habits to Build

- Drink at least 64 ounces of water per day, if not more.
- Eliminate sweets, fast food, and processed foods.
- Give thanks to God before meals.
- Meal prep for the week.
- Periodic fasting or cleanses.

HEARING

Your hearing is sharper for God's voice and the needs of others. Now this is both physical and spiritual, as you can "hear" God's voice when it is not audible. But that is for another time or another book. I love hearing worship music because it's one of my biggest passions in life, especially leading worship with my angelic-voiced wife. Music entertains me, it edifies me, it encourages me, it soothes me, it calms me, and so much more. How powerful is that? One sense can do so much for our spiritual well-being. However, similar to sight, what you let in has a significant impact on your life and spiritual well-being. If you listen to angry screaming metal, or F-bomb dropping anti-female rap music, or podcasts that don't do anything but tear down (politics pretty much), your life will not benefit.

Hearing Habits to Build

- Morning worship.
- Positive podcasts to learn, educate, and inspire.
- Family conversations.
- Sound fast. It's ok to be silent.
- Curate a playlist.

SMELL

Your smell helps you create healthy environments. This can be more of an "atmosphere" thing. Set the atmosphere in your home with candles, flowers, or plants. Do the dishes and take out the trash to ensure your environment is clean and odor-free. That affects you. I'm not a snake oil advocate, but there is something to be said about using essential oils, either on your skin or in a diffuser. Again, setting the atmosphere to pray, worship, minister, disciple, and learn is of understated importance in our lives.

Smell Habits to Build

- Open the windows in your house or car in the morning and breathe in the fresh air. Or again, go outside.
- Use essential oils, fresh herbs, and spices when cooking.

- Aromatherapy baths.
- Take up gardening or caring for plants in your home.
- Remove unwanted negative smells and replace them with clean, fresh ones.

TOUCH

Touch allows you to comfort and serve others effectively. The bible says we are His hands and feet. We were created to reach out and touch other people. Sorry, introverts, but that Sunday morning greeting time with your neighbor is so important. Touching, feeling, hugging, and embracing are such important needs in our lives, whether we want to admit it or not.

Sometimes, a hug when you're sad, or lonely, or depressed can completely turn your day around. I believe that your exercise routine should be included here. Your willingness to work out, walk, or run has everything to do with you touching something that will benefit your body. And, I'll just say it, if you're married...have sex. God designed it. It is good.

Touch Habits to Build

- Morning stretching or exercise.
- Technology breaks, away from your keyboard.
- Serve others by cooking or cleaning.
- Hug one person each day.
- Give way more high-fives. Who doesn't like a high-five?

Remember: These habits aren't about perfection; they're about intentionally stewarding the amazing sensory gifts God has given you to experience His creation and serve others effectively.

Your five senses aren't accidents. They're intentional gifts from the God who "fearfully and wonderfully made" you. Each sense serves both practical and spiritual purposes: your sight connects you to Scripture and beauty, your hearing tunes you to God's voice and encouragement, your taste guides proper nutrition and gratitude, your smell creates atmospheres for worship and peace, and your touch allows you to comfort and serve others effectively. When you steward these senses well through simple daily habits, you're not just improving your health; you're honoring the Designer of your temple and optimizing your ability to fulfill His calling on your life.

This week, choose one sense and implement one new habit. Perhaps it's scripture before screens for your eyesight, or morning worship music for your ears, or drinking more water and eliminating one processed food item. Start small, stay consistent, and remember that every sensory choice is either honoring or dishonoring the temple God gave you.

Your body is the vehicle for every calling God has placed on your life. When your senses are sharp and your temple is strong, you have the energy to pursue your purpose, the stamina to serve others, and the longevity to see your legacy fulfilled.

Don't just read about sensory stewardship. Start practicing today. Your future self will thank you, and more importantly, your Creator will be honored through the way you care for His masterpiece.

🔘 Renew4D Reflection: Making Sense of Your Body

Discover the lie you've believed.

You may have believed your body is separate from your spiritual walk, or worse, that it no longer matters because of age, pain, or past neglect. But your body is the temple of the Holy Spirit. It's not just a vehicle; it's a vessel. What you feel, sense, and experience physically has direct spiritual implications. The lie is that you can ignore your body and still fully walk in your calling. The truth? You are fearfully and wonderfully made—and still responsible for stewarding that design.

Develop truth-based rhythms for physical renewal.

- "Your body is a temple of the Holy Spirit." – 1 Corinthians 6:19
- "You were bought with a price. Therefore, honor God with your body." – 1 Corinthians 6:20
- "You are fearfully and wonderfully made." – Psalm 139:14
- "Take care of your body. It's the only place you have to live." – Jim Rohn

Use your five God-given senses to guide daily stewardship of your health and awareness. Start small. Stack new habits onto old ones. Let every sensory experience remind you of your Creator's goodness.

Deploy simple, sensory-based habits to steward your body.

This isn't about trying to be a CrossFit champion. This is about intentionality. Honor God with what you see, hear, taste, smell, and touch, because each of those inputs influences your health, your mood, your focus, and your ability to serve.

Sample Sensory Habit Stacks:

• **Sight**: Scripture before screens; 15 minutes of morning sunlight

• **Hearing**: Worship while cooking; positive podcast during your commute

• **Taste**: Drink water before meals; fast from sugar 1 day/week

• **Smell**: Diffuse calming oils while journaling or praying

• **Touch**: Hug a loved one daily; stretch after brushing teeth; walk after dinner

Habit Tip: Steward your senses. Don't silence them.

God designed your senses for connection, worship, and mission. When you numb them with overstimulation or underuse, you miss out on both health and holiness. Don't aim for perfect routines, aim for consistent reverence.

Duplicate this lifestyle by modeling physical and spiritual discipline.

Let your kids see you stretch, pray, and praise. Let your friends know you're not on a diet, you're stewarding your temple. Let your marriage be refreshed by physical touch, shared meals, and sacred rest. The people around you don't need your perfection; they need your example.

13. THE PHYSICAL REPRESENTS THE SPIRITUAL

Your physical condition is a mirror reflecting your spiritual discipline. Just as you can't fake spiritual maturity, you can't fake physical health. The habits that build a strong body are the same habits that build a strong faith: consistency, sacrifice, delayed gratification, and the willingness to do what's right even when you don't feel like it.

If you're reading this as a mid-lifer in pain, carrying extra weight, or struggling with low energy, here's the truth: your physical struggles aren't separate from your spiritual calling; they're limiting it. You can't run the race Paul describes in *1 Corinthians 9:24* if your temple is crumbling. But here's the hope: the same God who can renew your spirit can restore your strength.

How the 4 D's Apply to Your Physical Health:

DISCOVER: What your body truly needs for energy, strength, and longevity versus what culture tells you

DEVELOP: Sustainable nutrition and exercise habits that fit your real life, not a fitness influencer's

DEPLOY: Consistent daily disciplines that compound into lifelong health and vitality

DUPLICATE: Modeling physical stewardship for your family and mentoring others in temple care

Why Physical Health Matters for Your Calling:

Every great spiritual leader in Scripture had to steward their physical strength for their mission. Moses climbed mountains at 120 years old. David fought giants. Jesus walked thousands of miles in His ministry. Your body isn't holding you back from your calling—it's supposed to be the vehicle that carries you through it. When you're physically strong, you have the energy to serve, the stamina to persevere, and the longevity to finish well.

What You'll Accomplish:

By the end of this chapter, you'll have a practical roadmap for nutrition that fuels rather than depletes you, exercise that strengthens rather than exhausts you, and daily habits that build the physical foundation your calling requires. You'll move from making excuses about your age to making investments in your future.

The work you put in now determines whether you'll be playing with your grandchildren or watching from a wheelchair. The choices you make today will determine whether you'll have the energy for your calling at 70 or if you'll be too weak to serve effectively.

It's time to stop managing decline and start building strength. Your future self and your calling depend on it.

<u>WARNING: I Am Not A Health Coach</u>

Please raise your left hand and put your right hand over your heart. Now, repeat after me.

"I...state your name...will not hold anything Jessee says in the upcoming chapter as fact, the "way", or as scientific truth that needs to be upheld. Everything stated is 100% opinion, and what worked for HIM. It may not work for ME, or even be safe in my situation. I will do my due diligence and research and/or consult my doctor before I do or take anything mentioned."

Now that we've got that out of the way, let me tell you a story about podcasts, books, nutrition, diet, and getting off medication.

Nutrition

I began 2025 with a goal in mind. Eat healthy and get my diet in order. I know, that's not a very SMART goal. Clearly, it bites me in the butt down the road. However, as of January 1, 2025, I began implementing some lifestyle changes.

In my hours of drive time, I listened to a hundred different podcasts. They ranged from political to inspirational, spiritual to business, and even some health specialists. It started with a Joe Rogan podcast that featured Gary Brecka. I'll save you the long scientific explanation that I'll just botch anyway, and say this. He talked about the "bio hack" of hydrogen water, salt, and nutrition. What he said resonated with me, because I was at a point of wanting to get off my personal anti-depressant medication. From what I've heard, it sounds like nutrition could be a key factor. And, it was.

I bought in. Literally, I bought the Echo hydrogen water bottle, H2 tabs, Baja sea salt, and the Body Health Perfect Amino. I knew investing in myself now would have long-term ROI. I needed my health under control now, so I could continue to play with my kids pain-free, dance with my daughter at her wedding, and play with my grandkids.

Later, I listened to more podcasts featuring leading biohackers, nutritionists, neurobiologists, and health scientists. People like Mark Hyman, Andrew Huberman, and Max Luagvere. I read some books, like Genius Foods. These people began to change my mindset on health. It wasn't just failed diets or missed exercise days. It began at the very core of your physical being. Nutrition, vitamins, minerals. The very things your body makes and needs, and that you now don't have enough of because of our lifestyle, work style, and overly processed and sugary foods being 60-70% of the average American's diet, if not more, especially for young kids...hello Kellogg's and Red Bull.

I was already taking a myriad of supplements, along with my doctor-prescribed medication. Along with still recovering from back surgery, I had vitamins, supplements, protein, anti-depressants, muscle relaxers, and pain meds all inside me. I just felt gross.

I don't remember who, possibly Mark Hyman, mentioned an app called SuppCo. It's a supplement app that rates your vitamins and supplements. It's an all-in-one companion app that turns supplements from confusing and questionable into clear, trustworthy, and personalized. It allows you to schedule, supp stack, and more. But most importantly, it provides a "trust score" for the actual manufacturer, based on a list of credentials such as third-party testing, manufacturing process, and more. Aka, does the label match what's actually in the bottle?

There were supplements and vitamins that I was taking that were awful. Terrile scores. Not trustworthy. Not what I needed to be ingesting. They certainly weren't aiding my mental health and body change.

This app allowed me to find specific protocols tailored to me, such as weight management and men over 40. I found supplements that were good for my NAFLD (Non-Alcoholic Fatty Liver Disease). All the pain meds from my back surgery had taken a toll on my liver numbers and bloodwork. I found relatively cheap supplements to tackle my liver issues and fill in the gaps to restore its numbers and functionality.

I learned the importance of stacking certain supplements together, such as omega-3 fish oil, magnesium, and vitamin D3 + K2. Long story short, and a few extra dollars later, I found myself in June of 2025, 6 months later, throwing away all of my anti-depressant meds and even my statins. And yes, I consulted my doctor and followed a regimen to wean myself off. I didn't just throw it away and move on.

Proper nutrition helped improve my gut health, mental well-being, liver function, and cholesterol levels. I am one to believe that LDL is NOT the sole reason for heart issues. In fact, it's the opposite, sort of. But I'll let you do a little investigative work to go down that rabbit hole.

I'll go over my morning routine and supplement stack later in the resources section.

In just six months, I went from an overwhelmed, overmedicated dad recovering from surgery to someone finally taking ownership of his health, starting at the cellular level. What began as a vague goal to "eat healthy" became a deep dive into functional nutrition, podcast rabbit holes, and smarter supplementation.

With the help of experts like Gary Brecka and Mark Hyman, and tools like the SuppCo app, I eliminated low-quality vitamins, targeted my NAFLD, stabilized my mental health, and improved my liver and cholesterol levels. I didn't just feel better; I was Renew4D, inside and out.

This wasn't a quick fix. It was a complete shift, stacked supplements, morning routines, and slow, intentional changes that added up.

"Eat healthy" sounds great… until you try to actually do it. If you've ever made a vague health goal, downloaded a dozen apps, or stood in the supplement aisle wondering what "bioavailable" even means, you're not alone. That's where the Four D's come in. They turned my nutrition journey from overwhelming to intentional. And they can do the same for you.

Discover in Nutrition
This is where you stop lying to yourself.

You recognize that food isn't just fuel, it's emotional, habitual, cultural, and sometimes chemical. I discovered how much my gut health, mental state, and energy were tied to what I was (and wasn't) putting in my body. I also discovered just how much junk I was consuming in the name of "convenience" or "comfort." Most of us have no idea how many additives, sugars, and nutrient gaps we're living with until we look closer.

Develop in Nutrition
Here's where clarity replaces chaos.

Once I stopped guessing and started learning from podcasts, experts, and trial and error, I began building a plan. I found tools that helped me track quality (like SuppCo), routines that provided consistency (like my morning "supp shake"), and supplements that actually met my needs. You don't need to master everything overnight; you just need to start building more intelligent systems.

Deploy in Nutrition
This is where action replaces excuses.

I didn't overhaul my entire life in a weekend. I made a few small adjustments, such as my hydration, supplement timing, and morning routine, and let those compound. You don't need to be perfect. Just keep showing up. Every meal is a new chance to nourish yourself. Every morning is a reset.

Duplicate in Nutrition
This is where you create your new normal.

Once I figured out what worked, specific protocols for men over 40, targeted support for my liver, and a real rhythm, I just kept doing it. I stopped chasing trends and started repeating the things that actually made me feel alive again. This is where change becomes sustainable. And more importantly, this is where you become an "expert" enough to start sharing with others, and trying to help your friends or family who are struggling with their weight, diet, and nutrition.

Nutrition isn't about restriction, it's about restoration. Discover what your body actually needs. Develop a simple plan. Deploy with consistency. Duplicate what works.

Now that the foundation is set, it's time to talk food. Because the real transformation? It starts in the kitchen.

<u>Diet</u>

My weight has been a literal roller coaster the past 5 years. I've gone through seasons of intense and closely monitored dieting, thanks to apps like Yuka (to verify the nutritional value of the food I was eating) and MyFitnessPal (to track calories, food intake, and weight changes).

This is the hardest section to write about in this entire book. It's because I LOVE FOOD. I love Sonic ice cream. I love Taco Bell. I love Viking Pizza in my town. I love terrible cereal. And, it's so easy to be lazy now that we can claim being "tired' and just order Door Dash, and from what should have been some chicken and peppers turned into a quesadilla and wings from Applebee's.

This is the most challenging section, because it's the one I struggle with the most. As I write this page, I'm in the same battle I've fought many times before.

Growing up, I was a chunky kid. Then I grew by a foot one summer. I didn't lose weight, I just stretched out. Then I was super skinny for most of my youth and young adult ages. As I got older, things slowed, like my metabolism. I moved to the south (home of fried foods, BBQ, and cobbler). I got married. I had kids. And thus...the ultimate dad bod was created. The problem was, though, that yes, round is a figure, but I wasn't the father figure I wanted to be. I've lost 20-30 pounds several times, only to gain it all back quickly. Up and down. Throw out old clothes. Buy new ones 6 months later because I've gained weight again.

Before my back surgery, it was a real wake-up call. Freshly 40, I knew I needed to make a change. I knew I needed to lose weight if I had any chance to survive my back surgery and get back on my feet. I joined a meal prep program that sent me food (for a very pretty penny). It worked. I was extremely diligent in following the rules. The problem is, I couldn't maintain it. I couldn't afford the meals, and as soon as I was off, I tried my hardest to replicate them and their structure, but it didn't work out. I gained weight instantly. It wasn't sustainable.

I joined Plant Fitness. That was great for a while. I could feel muscles for the first time in a decade. I'm not sure if that helped my back pain or not. But it didn't last. The drive was "too far", or my schedule with kids and work didn't work with driving to the gym. Same excuses you've probably said.

I walked every morning at 5 am with a group of men in my neighborhood. That was honestly the best exercise I've ever done. It was easy, allowed me to commune with fellow men and believers, and it did work up a sweat and burn calories.

But again, it failed. We stopped walking, and I didn't continue by myself. I lost close to 40 pounds before my back surgery. I looked and felt amazing. The best I've felt in over a decade. That's what I want again. That's what I want my "normal" to be. What I lacked back then was the Four D's. If you're a mid-life dad, I'm guessing you might be in the same boat as me. So here is a quick breakdown of how the Four D's can help you stay on track with your diet and weight. FYI...I am currently in this phase. So I'm with you. You're not alone on this journey.

Discover in Dieting

This is where most of us begin, reacting to pain or frustration. You discovered your current patterns: emotional eating, failed diets, the ease of convenience food, and the more profound emotional attachment to food (comfort, reward, nostalgia). You also recognized the cycle: lose weight → feel better → lose routine → gain it back. This step isn't about shame, it's about becoming aware of what's really going on.

Dieting isn't just about food; it's about identity, environment, and sustainability. You really need a strong WHY here. You need to know WHY you're dieting and exercising. For me, it's for my wife and kids, and future grandkids. My family has a history of cancer, bone issues, and heart issues. I need to rewrite my family's future.

Develop in Dieting

This is where intention meets structure. It's where you stop setting vague goals, like "eat better," and instead build a SMART goal framework: Specific, Measurable, Achievable, Relevant, and Time-bound.

Instead of:

> "I want to lose weight."

You shift to:

> "I want to lose 12 pounds in the next 8 weeks by following a high-protein meal plan, walking 5x/week, and tracking meals in MyFitnessPal."

This is where you build rhythms, such as your morning walk, adopting a hydration-first mindset, or establishing a supplement stack routine. These are keystone habits that support long-term change.

Deploy in Dieting

This is the action stage. You start showing up, even imperfectly. You meal prep (or at least plan). Remember the Three D's of goal setting (A/B/C Goals). You set grocery boundaries. You prioritize movement. ***You allow grace without sliding into guilt.*** You experiment. You adjust. You keep going.

This is where you realized things like:
- Meal prep delivery worked, but wasn't sustainable
- The gym helped, but the location limited consistency
- Morning walks were both effective and spiritually refreshing. And instead of letting failure stop you, you learned from it.

"Deploy isn't about perfect execution, it's about imperfect, faithful progress."

- Jessee Lovaas

Duplicate in Dieting
Now, take what worked and refine it.

- Can you find a budget-friendly version of the meal prep you liked?
- Can you recreate the community accountability from those morning walks?
- Can you adjust your workout expectations to fit your season?

And most importantly, can you make this your new normal? Not a sprint. Not a season. But a sustainable lifestyle built around health, purpose, and freedom?

I've failed enough times to know this isn't about another short-term diet or hype-fueled routine. I need more than motivation; I need a framework. That's why I'm applying the Four D's.

I'm learning to Discover what drives my habits, Develop rhythms that actually work for me, Deploy small changes with consistency, and Duplicate the things that stick, so my normal becomes a lifestyle I can be proud of.

Now that the fuel is in place, it's time to move. Because real strength? It's built in motion.

Exercise

If diet is the 1.a hardest section to write about, exercise is the 1.b. Similar to dieting, my exercise habits and routines were an equal rollercoaster of amazingness and detrimental failure. I've been to the gym. I've done YouTube routines to exercise in my room. I've downloaded plans to exercise using resistance bands. Currently, I have a brand-new weight bench and dumbbells by my bed that I bought last Christmas and have used only four times. Trust me, I do everything in my power to keep my "father figure". That is, nothing. I do nothing. Or rather, I DID nothing.

I actually enjoy exercising. I loved pumpkin iron at Planet Fitness. I loved walking in the mornings with the men in my neighborhood. However, exercising solo with no one around is where I tend to lose motivation. It's easy to exercise in a community. But will your WHY overpower your need for community to keep exercising and staying active, when others quit or stop? That's the million-dollar question.

One thing I absolutely fell in love with during this season was cold plunging. Or for me, the coldest shower possible. It was invigorating. I loved it. I became addicted to it. It woke me up, got my endorphins and blood flowing, and aided in my rucking and back recovery. It really was a drug I never knew I needed. One day, I'll have a tub with a water temperature controller.

That's where the Four D's come in. They've helped me reframe fitness, not as a guilt-driven obligation, but as a structured path I can actually follow.

Discover in Exercise
This is where you get honest.

What actually works for you? What doesn't? I've discovered that I enjoy exercising, but I hate doing it alone. I loved walking with the guys in my neighborhood. I loved lifting at Planet Fitness. But when that community faded, so did my drive. I wasn't lazy, I just needed more than willpower. Who do you know that can support you, or be an accountability partner to help you stay on course?

Develop in Exercise
This is where you build a realistic plan.

You don't need a gym membership, a 90-day program, or an overpriced app. You need a repeatable rhythm. For me, it was morning walks, short resistance circuits, and setting the bar low enough that I could actually hit it. What matters is consistency, not complexity.

Maybe you didn't realize how far you've come...

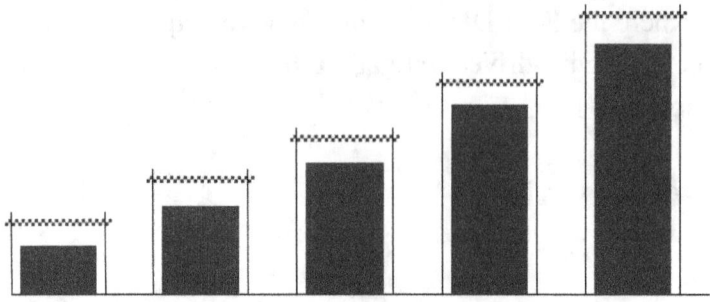

Because you keep raising the bar.

Deploy in Exercising

This is where action beats excuses.

It's easy to move when you feel motivated. The challenge is showing up when no one's watching. This is the grind, the part where your WHY has to be stronger than your comfort. Not perfect, just honest effort. Ten minutes count just as much as a walk around the block. Keep going. One day, you'll look back, in hindsight, and see just how far you've really come.

Duplicate in Exercising

This is where you reinforce what sticks.

Don't reinvent the wheel; repeat what worked. Did you love walking with others? Start a group. Felt good after a quick lift? Put it on your calendar. This is how routines become a part of your lifestyle. This is how change becomes normal.

You don't need a new body. You need a Renew4D mindset. One step. One rep. One walk at a time.

This chapter isn't just about health tips; it's about alignment. The physical and spiritual are not separate tracks; they're intertwined.

How you treat your body reflects how you steward your purpose. Through my own story of injury, supplements, failed diets, and finding rhythms that actually work, I've discovered that getting healthy isn't about quick fixes; it's about building a life you don't have to recover from.

My Daily Morning Routine
(At least my Drive A-Goal)

1. Wake up at 5:00 am
2. Get my hydrogen water, with salt and electrolytes (sometimes just LMNT)
3. Ruck/Walk for 30 minutes
4. Drink another 32 ounces of water upon return
5. Cold plunge shower
6. Pause for 5 minutes to set the atmosphere
7. Read, pray, and journal
8. Read at least 1 chapter of a book
9. Supplement Shake
10. COFFEE

The Four D's (Discover, Develop, Deploy, Duplicate) offered me a framework for reclaiming my physical health through nutrition, diet, and exercise. I learned to stop guessing and start fueling my body intentionally. I confronted the emotional and cultural baggage around food. I redefined movement as something life-giving, not performance-driven. And I built systems, not streaks.

Your body isn't a burden. It's the vehicle for your calling. You were made to finish strong. Whether you're carrying extra weight, low energy, chronic pain, or just the frustration of trying and failing again, know that you're not stuck. You're not too late. You're not alone.

It's time to stop managing your decline and start building your future. Your health is not about abs, it's about access. Access to your full energy. Access to your mission. Access to the moments that matter most. Now let's build a body that can carry the weight of your calling.

Renew4D Reflection: The Physical Represents the Spiritual

Discover the lie you've believed.

Maybe you've believed that your physical health is separate from your spiritual life. That gaining weight, feeling tired, or ignoring your body is just "normal" in midlife. However, the truth is that your body reflects your spirit. Just like you can't fake spiritual maturity, you can't fake physical health. What you neglect in the natural will eventually impact the supernatural. The lie says, "It's too late." The truth says, "Start today and watch God restore."

Develop truth-based habits of physical stewardship.

- "Do you not know that your body is the temple of the Holy Spirit?" - *1 Corinthians 6:19*
- "Run in such a way that you may obtain the prize." - *1 Corinthians 9:24*
- "Honor God with your body." - *1 Corinthians 6:20*

Your nutrition, exercise, and daily decisions aren't about image; they're about integrity. Start with systems, not streaks. Fuel your body, move consistently, and build a foundation that supports your spiritual calling.

Deploy daily disciplines that match the weight of your calling.

Nutrition isn't about restriction. Exercise isn't about performance. Health is about capacity, the capacity to parent well, serve others with energy, and say yes to the calling God has placed on your life. Whether it's your "supp shake," walking group, or morning stretch, keep showing up. Let small, intentional steps become your new normal.

⚒ Habit Tip: Stack habits that serve your future self.

Don't try to overhaul your life overnight. Stack new health habits (like hydration, meal prep, or movement) onto routines you already do. Utilize tools like SuppCo, MyFitnessPal, and habit-tracking journals to establish a structured routine. Focus less on willpower and more on rhythm. Faithfulness compounds.

Duplicate your Renew4D health by modeling and mentoring.

Let your spouse, kids, and community see what physical stewardship looks like. Share what's working. Invite others to join you on your walks or share in your meal plans. Be a living example that health isn't about six-packs, it's about showing up energized for your life's mission. Don't wait for perfection. Start with progress.

⧗ Final Challenge:
Pick ONE area, nutrition, diet, or exercise, and apply the Four D's this week.

Maybe it's:
- **Nutrition**: Start your day with a "supp shake" before coffee
- **Diet**: Track food in MyFitnessPal for 5 days
- **Exercise**: Take a 10-minute walk each morning before work

Every step strengthens your temple. Every habit rebuilds your energy. Your body isn't separate from your calling. It's what carries it. You don't need to become an athlete. You just need to become aligned.

Section Wrap-Up: Review & Reflection

What did you DISCOVER about your body?

_____

_____

_____

_____

What will you begin to DEVELOP in your body?

_____

_____

_____

_____

What will you DEPLOY in your life and your body?

_____

_____

_____

_____

What will DUPLICATE and teach someone else about the body?

_____

_____

_____

_____

CELEBRATION TIME

You just discovered the blueprint for body transformation! You didn't just read about health, you learned that your body is the temple of the Holy Spirit, and you now have the tools to steward it with intentionality, energy, and purpose. You understand how your five senses connect to your calling, how nutrition, movement, and habit stacking restore your strength, and how physical renewal unlocks access to the mission God placed on your life. That's massive progress worth celebrating right now.

Put this book down and go celebrate. Drink a glass of water and thank God for your body. Go for a walk and breathe in the fresh air. Call someone and share your biggest breakthrough from these chapters. Start your first habit stack today. Maybe it's scripture before screens or stretching after you brush your teeth. Your excitement for whole-body renewal is contagious, and when you model what you've learned, you invite others to do the same. And just maybe...get a scoop of ice cream. You've earned it!

Don't put off being happy for the sake of growing and grinding.

PART 6

ADVENTURE TIME

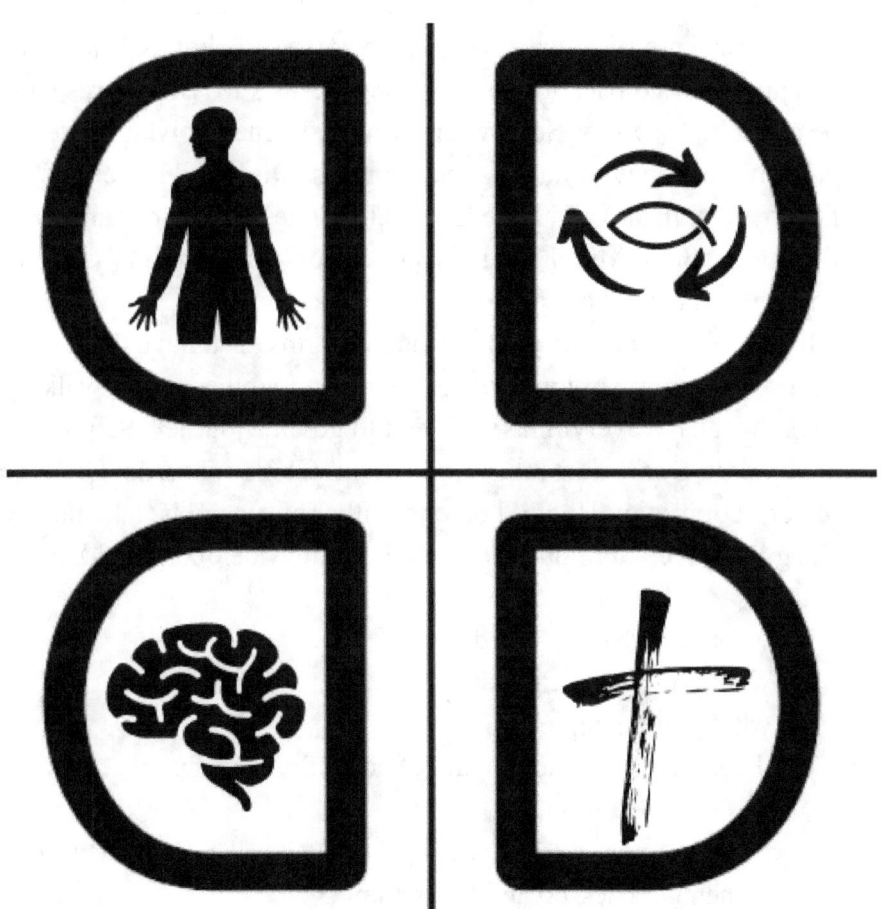

14. HANDS & FEET

We are rounding third and heading for home. The final two chapters remain. This chapter sets the tone for your upcoming journey. The final chapter...well, that's a surprise. If you made it this far and read the final chapter, I'll give you a little bonus. Stay tuned.

Again, let's go back to the beginning. Jesus's **FINAL** words should be our **FIRST** works. So now that you've learned how to arhitec your life in a new way, using the Four D's (Discover, Develop, Deploy, Duplicate) and have thoroughly ingested the four areas of life (Body, Soul, Mind, Spirit), you can now put them into your backpack and head out on your magical adventure.

Imagine yourself like young Frodo Baggins. You have the One Ring, your supply rations, a spare change of clothes, and a walking stick. You have everything you need to go on a journey. So go. Now! Don't wait. Don't waste this momentum. Go now, and do. Don't wait in your comfy tiny Hobbit home to wither away and be taken by the Nazgul. Leave your house and step into the wide open world, and do.

Do what you've discovered.
Do what you've developed.
Do what you've deployed.
Duplicate it all, and do it again. And again. And again.

And when you get tired or weary. Stop, take a break, have a little snack. Then get back up and keep doing.

"So whether you eat or drink or whatever you do, do it all for the glory of God."

- 1 Corinthians 10:31

Let your transformation be a daily act of worship, not just a matter of willpower. Now that you've Renew4D your life, there's no better way to glorify the Creator than to share it with someone else, or to help someone else renew their life.

It is our job, as leaders, as Christians, as men and women, mothers and fathers, to help others. It is our job to lead others into a brighter tomorrow. How can we effectively help anyone if we are battered and broken? We can't. We need renewal. We need our entire lives to be radically Renew4D, restored, and changed. Our lives depend on it. But more so, the lives of others depend on us.

Climb That Mountain

Paul's message in *1 Corinthians 12* reminds us that every believer is part of one body, and every part has a divine purpose. You weren't randomly created. You were placed, strategically, intentionally, and purposefully, by God to fulfill a role no one else can. When you fully embrace your identity as part of His body, you also embrace your responsibility to function within that body, not for yourself, but for the good of others.

But how do you know where you're meant to serve?

That's where the 7 Mountains of Influence come in. Family, Faith, Education, Government, Business, Arts & Entertainment, and Media. These spheres shape culture. And God doesn't call everyone to the same one. Some are called to minister in the church, while others are called to minister in the classroom, the boardroom, or the courtroom. But every mountain needs the light of Jesus carried by people who know who they are and why they're there.

Discovering your gifting and calling is how you begin to see where God is asking you to be His hands and feet. When you understand your role in the body of Christ, whether as an "eye" for vision, a "hand" for action, or a "foot" for movement, you can begin climbing the mountain you're assigned to, carrying the gospel with you, and sharing your Renew4D life.

Your gifting isn't random.
Your passions aren't accidents.
Your story wasn't wasted.

They are all clues to your calling.

And when you step into your mountain of influence with a Renew4D life, you aren't going in alone. You're going as a representative of Christ, a member of His body, carrying His heart into places that desperately need it, into ANY sphere of influence.

This is what it means to be Renew4D. Not just personally transformed, but deployed with purpose. When the body of Christ shows up in every mountain, culture begins to shift. Not because of domination, but because of restoration, because the body is finally working as one.

Your hands might be the ones God uses to lift someone up. Your voice might be the one that speaks hope. Your feet might be the ones that carry the gospel into someone's mess. You are not only part of the body of Christ. He encourages you to take action.

Just don't give up trying. Someone's hardship might be too hard to break through at first. Still, I promise, if you continue to live a Renew4D life, share it, and lead by example, being empathetic and compassionate, while building relationships, then you will see that hardship turns into a new disciple, ready to start discipling others themselves.

"Never give in. Never give in. Never, never, never, never, in nothing, great or small, large or petty, never give in, except to convictions of honour and good sense."

- Winston Churchill

It's not just about blind stubbornness. Churchill's deeper wisdom is that we stand unwaveringly on truth and principle, and that we never quit in the pursuit of what's right, whether we're fighting tyranny or pursuing personal growth.

I highly doubt you're facing tyranny, but personal growth is possibly the most complex and challenging battlefield you'll ever encounter.

Share your journey with others. Invite others into your life, into your home. Give them a "peek behind the curtain." My current pastor says, "Empty tables are for interviews and interrogations. Full tables are for community and family."

Your personal life, your home, and your table are where life happens and relationships grow.

You've come a long way. Body, soul, mind, and spirit Renew4D, and now you're standing at the edge of purpose. This chapter is your call to action. It's your Frodo moment. With the Four D's in your backpack and your identity firmly rooted in Christ, it's time to step out and climb the mountain God designed for you. Whether that mountain is in business, education, government, faith, family, media, or the arts, your life was never meant to stay safely tucked away in Hobbiton. It was meant to go.

This chapter challenges you to step into your gifting, embrace your role in the body of Christ, and boldly bring renewal to your sphere of influence. Because your story, your scars, your passions, they're not random. They're clues to your calling. And when you show up, Renew4D, culture begins to shift. So don't wait for perfection. Don't overthink the next step. Just go. Do. Live. Share. Repeat.

15. Bonus 5th D

You made it. Thank you for reading 15 chapters of my life's testimony so far, which includes the scars, trials, hardships, difficulties, failures, wins, victories, and accomplishments. You've now read my dream. You've now participated in duplicating Jessee. And for that, I owe you the world. Thank you for trusting me to go this far. Thank you for allowing me to join you through 15 chapters and however many hours or days it took you to read this.

So I'm going to reward you with a little something special. A bonus 5th D. Are you ready? Get ready. I want you to **DREAM**.

DREAM

After you Discover your identity, Develop the habits, Deploy your gifts, and Duplicate your life into others, there comes a moment where you have to Dream. Dream bigger than before. Dream beyond your current circumstances. Dream the dreams God planted in your heart before fear talked you out of them.

This 5th D isn't about careful planning, it's about God-sized vision. It's where your renewed identity meets unlimited possibility. Where your developed skills become the foundation for something greater.

Dream of the impact you could have. Dream of the legacy you want to leave. Dream of the person you're becoming through this Renew4d life.

Here is some scriptural firepower to encourage you to dream with confidence, boldness, and divine vision:

- **Joel 2:28** - "I will pour out my Spirit on all people... your old men will dream dreams, your young men will see visions."
- **Jeremiah 29:11** - "For I know the plans I have for you," declares the Lord, "plans to prosper you and not to harm you, to give you hope and a future."
- **Ephesians 3:20** - "Now to him who is able to do immeasurably more than all we ask or imagine, according to his power that is at work within us."
- **Proverbs 29:18** - "Where there is no vision, the people perish."

How do you feel after reading those passages? Hopeful? Inspired? Like God has bigger plans for your life than you ever imagined? You should.

Once you discover your identity in God, develop your gifts, deploy them into your calling, and share your dreams with others, you can begin to inspire others to dream as well. Help them envision their own Renew4d life—body, soul, mind, and spirit.

"All our dreams can come true if we have the courage to pursue them."

- Walt Disney

We aren't supposed to live small, limited lives. We're called to live with vision, purpose, and divine imagination. We are called to be people who dream God-sized dreams and then watch Him make them reality.

The 5th D is about getting bold with your vision. Bold enough to dream out loud and inspire others to do the same. Think of it like planting seeds in a garden. Your renewed life is the soil, your dreams are the seeds, and God provides the growth.

When you live out your dreams, you give others permission to dream too. You show them what's possible when someone decides to stop settling and start believing.

What Dreaming Actually Looks Like For You

Many people think dreaming means unrealistic fantasies. But biblical dreaming is different. It looks like:

- Envisioning the business you've always wanted to start, and taking the first step
- Imagining yourself healthy and vibrant at 70, and making choices today to support that vision
- Seeing the impact you could have in your community, and volunteering for one cause
- Picturing the marriage you want to have, and having that conversation with your spouse
- Dreaming of the legacy you want to leave your children, and writing them a letter about it
- Visualizing yourself debt-free, and creating your first budget
- Imagining leading a small group or mentoring someone, and reaching out to your pastor
- Seeing yourself as an author, speaker, or leader, and writing your first blog post

Dreaming isn't just wishing, it's visioning with purpose. It's seeing what could be and then taking steps to make it a reality.

Create Your "Dream List"

Before you close this chapter, I want you to write out 3-5 dreams you will pursue in the next 30 days:

I dream of _____

I dream of _____

I dream of _____

I dream of _____

I dream of _____

Keep this list visible. Tape it to your bathroom mirror. Screenshot it. Text it to a friend. Then take one small step toward each dream, one at a time. And when you finish the list?

Dream bigger.

> *"The future belongs to those who believe in the beauty of their dreams."*

- Eleanor Roosevelt

Don't shrink your dreams to fit your fears.
Don't wait for perfect conditions.
Don't let others define what's possible for your life.
Don't live smaller than God designed you to.

You've been Renew4D. Now dream like it.

Dream of breaking generational cycles. Dream of building something beautiful with what you've been through. Dream of trying again, even if you failed before. Dream of living fully, leading boldly, and leaving nothing on the table.

"Now to him who is able to do immeasurably more than all we ask or imagine..."

- Ephesians 3:20

And when the time comes to hand off your legacy, may they say of you:

They didn't just survive—they thrived.

They didn't just exist—they dreamed.

They lived Renew4d. They Dreamed big.

16. Now What?

Journal.

That's what.

If you haven't yet—which I hope you have—I want you to get my **Renew4D 90-Day Journal**. Not just any journal. This one. Because everything you've just learned needs a place to live, grow, and compound.

You will not retain it without writing it, seeing it, meditating on it, and revisiting it — all while practicing it. Habakkuk 2:2 says, ***"Write the vision and make it plain on tablets, that he may run who reads it."*** It's hard to run after something that isn't written down or in front of you.

Here's a staggering truth: **92-95% of people who don't write down their goals never achieve them**. But here's the beautiful part—just by picking up a pen, you join the top 5% of people who take action. A 30-minute activity of writing sets you apart from 95% of people. How incredible is that!

Don't just write it down, though. Take it one step further and share it with someone. Even scarier? Invite someone into your journey. By including someone, you create accountability and another source of encouragement when you start falling short.

Your 90-Day Transformation Blueprint

The Renew4D 90-Day Journal isn't just pages with lines. It's your roadmap to renewal, designed around everything you've learned in this book. Here's how it works:

Why 90 Days?

Research shows it takes 66-90 days to form lasting habits. Quarterly cycles align with natural rhythms of goal setting. It gives you enough time to see real transformation while keeping you motivated with a clear finish line.

90 days from now, you will not be the same person.

The Three-Month Journey

Month 1: Foundation Building

- Complete brain dump of all your dreams and desires
- Set SMART goals for Body, Soul, Mind, and Spirit
- Identify current habits—good, bad, and new
- Map your Seven Mountains influence plan
- Begin daily Four D's practice

Month 2: Course Correction

- Evaluate and adjust your goals based on what you've learned
- Refine habits that are working, change ones that aren't
- Deepen your Seven Mountains impact
- Build momentum through weekly celebrations

Month 3: Final Push

- Focus on completion and legacy building
- Master the habits that will serve you beyond 90 days
- Prepare for your next level of influence
- Celebrate the incredible transformation you've achieved

Here's exactly what the Dreams & Goals Brain Dump looks like in your journal:

Write down everything on your heart—dreams, goals, desires, ambitions. Big or small, practical or wild. If it matters to you, write it down.

_____

_____

_____

What specific goals do you want to accomplish in the next 90 days?

_____

_____

_____

Here's exactly what the Habits Inventory looks like in your journal:

List your current habits—good ones to keep, bad ones to change, new ones to add.

HABITS TO KEEP:
(Body, Soul, Mind, Spirit - What's already working well?)

_____

_____

HABITS TO CHANGE/REMOVE:
(What's holding you back in any of the four areas?)

_____

_____

NEW HABITS TO ADD:
(What do you want to start doing for Body, Soul, Mind, Spirit?)

_____

_____

Your New Daily Rhythm

Remember the framework from this book? Here's how it becomes your daily practice:

Morning - Set intentions, review goals, connect with God
Midday - Pause, pray, reset your focus for the afternoon
Evening - Four D's reflection, habit tracking, gratitude

Each day in your journal, you'll answer these simple but powerful questions:

The Four D's Daily Check-In:

- **DISCOVER** - What's one thing you learned today?
- **DEVELOP** - What's one thing you practiced today?
- **DEPLOY** - What's one thing you overcame today?
- **DUPLICATE** - Who's one person you discipled today?

Your Four Life Areas Habit Tracker:

- **BODY HABIT** - What was your daily goal for your body, and did you achieve it?
- **SOUL HABIT** - What was your daily goal for your soul, and did you achieve it?
- **MIND HABIT** - What was your daily goal for your mind, and did you achieve it?
- **SPIRIT HABIT** - What was your daily goal for your spirit, and did you achieve it?

Setting Your SMART Goals (The Right Way)

After you complete your first month's brain dump and habit inventory, it's time to get specific with SMART Goals—one for each life area.

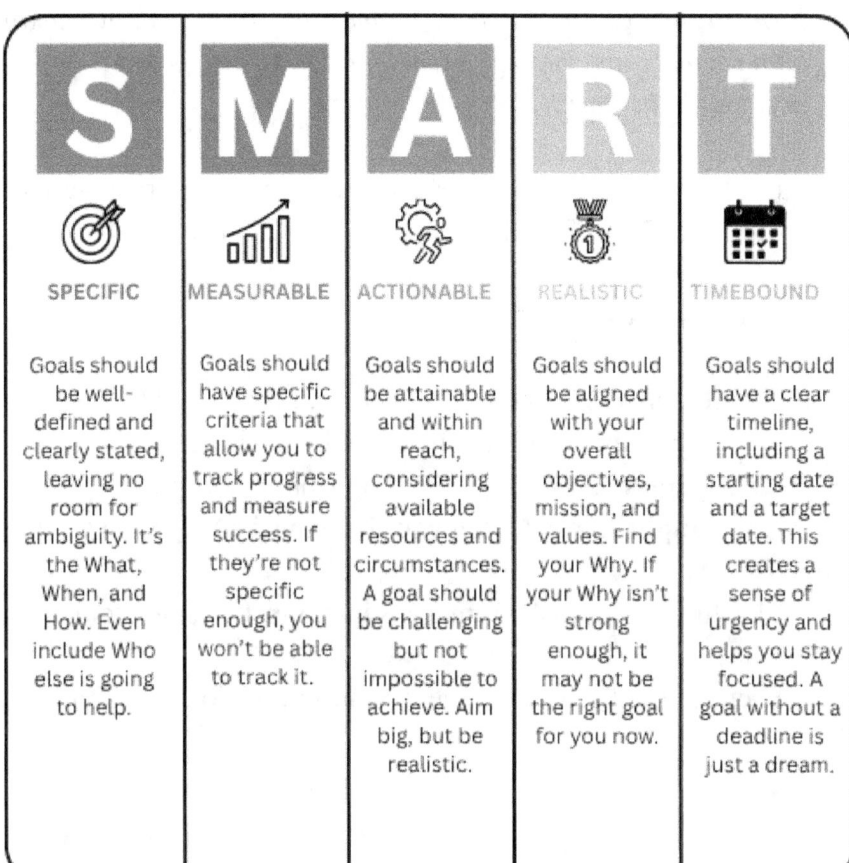

The SMART Framework:

- **Specific** – What exactly do you want to achieve?
- **Measurable** – How will you track progress?
- **Achievable** – Is this realistic with your time, energy, and resources?
- **Relevant** – Does this move you closer to your purpose or calling?
- **Time-bound** – Give your goal a clear deadline.

Use this format: *"I want to [do what] by [when], by [how], with [who]."*

Example: *"I want to lose 15 pounds by March 31st, by walking 30 minutes daily and cutting out fast food, with my spouse as my accountability partner."*

But here's what makes the Renew4D Journal different—after you write each SMART goal, you'll connect it to the Four D's:

The 4 D's Application:

- **Discover**: What will you learn along the way?
- **Develop**: What skills/habits will you practice?
- **Deploy**: How will you act on what you learn?
- **Duplicate**: Who will you share this journey with?

This turns your goals from tasks into transformation tools.

Each area of life's goal page in your journal looks like this:

BODY GOAL - Month 1

GOAL: I want to _____ by
_____ , by _____
with _____ .

WHY?:

_____
_____
_____

SMART CHECK:

☐ Specific ☐ Measurable ☐ Achievable ☐ Relevant ☐ Time-bound

THE 4 D'S: BODY AUDIT

Discover: What will you learn along the way?

_____

Develop: What skills/habits will you practice?

_____

Deploy: How will you act on what you learn?

_____

Duplicate: Who will you share this journey with?

_____

BONUS**

HABIT STACK: After I _____ ,
I will _____ .

The Seven Mountains Integration

Your journal includes a revolutionary addition—tracking your influence across the Seven Mountains of Culture:

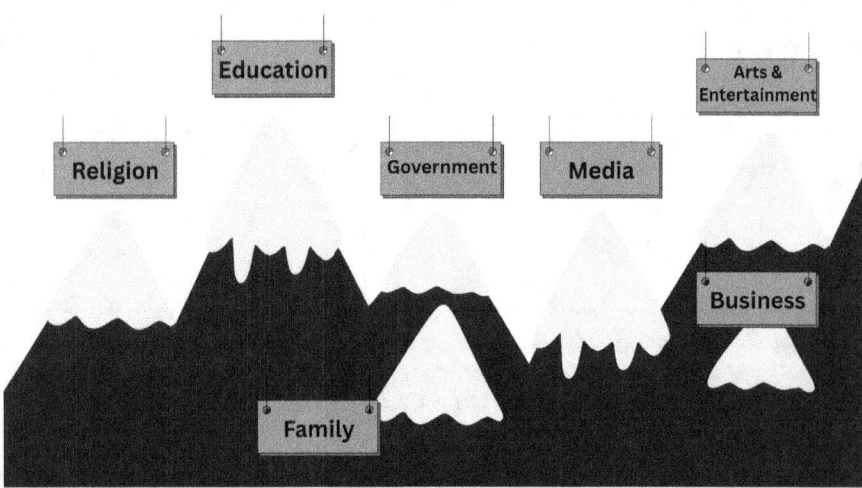

- **Family** – Your household influence
- **Religion** – Church and spiritual community
- **Education** – Learning and teaching
- **Media/Arts** – Communication and creativity
- **Entertainment** – Recreation and culture
- **Business** – Work and economy
- **Government** – Civic engagement

Each month, you'll assess and plan your impact in these areas. Because your renewal isn't just about you—it's about the influence you'll have on the world around you.

Your journal includes this dedicated page for mapping your cultural influence:

Seven Mountains Vision

How will you influence each mountain in the next 90 days?
Choose at least one, if not multiple. It's ok to skip some of these.

FAMILY:

_____
_____
_____

RELIGION:

_____
_____
_____

EDUCATION:

_____
_____
_____

MEDIA/ARTS:

_____
_____
_____

ENTERTAINMENT:

_____
_____
_____

BUSINESS:

_____
_____
_____

GOVERNMENT:

_____
_____

Weekly Celebrations (This Is Crucial!)

Here's something most goal-setting systems miss: **celebration**.

Every week, your journal includes celebration prompts. Don't just power through. Pause and celebrate. Even one change puts you in the top 5% of people who take action.

After completing your first week, celebrate!

- High-five your kids
- Hug your spouse
- Thank God for His faithfulness
- Call someone who's supporting you

You need to make a HUGE emphasis on celebrating your victories and taking joy in life. Don't let this become another "self-help system" that gives you more things to do. Do one thing and focus on that. When it becomes a habit, add another.

Monthly Reviews and Resets

Every 30 days, you'll pause and reflect:

- What habits are sticking?
- Which goals need adjustment?
- How are you impacting the Seven Mountains?
- What has God revealed about your calling?

Your goals will change—and that's beautiful! It means you're growing, learning, and being led by the Holy Spirit toward becoming who you are.

The Power of "Anything Above Zero"

Remember this phrase. Write it down. Live by it.

"Anything above zero compounds."

You won't hit every goal every day. You won't complete every habit perfectly. That's not the point. The point is showing up consistently, one day at a time, knowing that even small progress creates momentum.

Drank one extra glass of water? That compounds.
Prayed for five minutes instead of zero? That compounds.
Sent one encouraging text? That compounds.
Read one page instead of scrolling social media? That compounds.

Start Small, But Start Today

Simon Sinek said, *"Dream big. Start small. But most of all, start."*
Don't wait until Monday. Don't wait until next month. Don't wait until you have your life figured out.

Start today with something small:

Get up five minutes earlier ✓
Eat one healthy meal ✓
Read one page of Scripture ✓
Write down one goal ✓

"Slow and steady wins the race."

- a turtle 🐢

169

Your First Day Instructions

Here's exactly what to do when you get your Renew4D 90-Day Journal:

1. **Find a quiet place** with no distractions
2. **Pray for wisdom** - Ask God to guide this journey
3. **Complete the Month 1 goal-setting section** - Dreams, habits, Seven Mountains vision, SMART goals
4. **Celebrate** what you just accomplished (seriously, do this!)
5. **Set your alarm** for tomorrow's first daily entry
6. **Invite someone** into your journey for accountability

The Daily Rhythm in Action

Let me walk you through what a typical day looks like with your journal:

Morning (10-15 minutes):

- Write your daily intention
- Review your goals
- Connect with God through prayer or Scripture

Midday (5-10 minutes):

- Pause and pray
- Quick check-in: How am I doing on my priorities?
- Course correct if needed

Evening (10-15 minutes):

- Complete your Four D's reflection
- Check off your habit tracker

- End with gratitude or a win from the day

That's it. 20-30 minutes total spread across your day. Less time than you spend scrolling social media, but infinitely more life-changing.

Every day, you'll use this simple format:

DAILY JOURNAL

MORNING:

MIDDAY:

BEDTIME:

DISCOVER - What's one thing you learned today?

DEVELOP - What's one thing you practiced today?

DEPLOY - What's one thing you overcame today?

DUPLICATE - Who's one person you helped today?

HABIT TRACKER

What habit were you tracking today? Did you accomplish it?

BODY

Yes ◯
No ◯

SOUL

Yes ◯
No ◯

MIND

Yes ◯
No ◯

SPIRIT

Yes ◯
No ◯

GRATITUDE: End your day with **gratitude** or a **win** from today.

_____
_____
_____
_____

Why This Journal Changes Everything

This isn't just about tracking habits. It's about becoming who God made you to be while impacting the world around you.

Every day, you're:

- Aligning your life with God's purposes (**Spirit**)
- Renewing your thought patterns (**Mind**)
- Building character through habits (**Soul**)
- Stewarding your physical temple (**Body**)
- Influencing culture through the **Seven Mountains**

Daily introspection is the mirror that reveals who you're becoming. When you pause each day to reflect through the lens of the Four D's, you measure not just progress, but purpose.

The 90-Day Promise

Here's what I promise you: If you commit to this 90-day journey—really commit—you will not be the same person who started.

Your habits will compound. Your influence will expand. Your relationship with God will deepen. Your impact on the Seven Mountains will increase.

But more than that, you'll prove to yourself that lasting change is possible. That small steps lead to big transformations. That you have what it takes to become who God created you to be.

What Happens After 90 Days?

Start another 90 days.

The journey of renewal never ends. But now you'll have

momentum, proven systems, and the confidence that comes from already succeeding once.

Share your story. Someone needs to hear that transformation is possible. Your journey could be the spark that ignites theirs.

Keep living the Four D's. Continue to discover, develop, deploy, and duplicate. This framework will serve you for the rest of your life.

Your Assignment Right Now

Don't just read this and move on. Take action.

1. **Get the Renew4D 90-Day Journal** (seriously, stop making excuses)
2. **Schedule your first journaling session** - Put it in your calendar right now
3. **Tell someone** about your commitment to this journey
4. **Pray** and ask God to prepare your heart for transformation

Remember James 2:17: *"Faith without works is dead."* You have faith. You have goals. Now put action to them.

The Truth About Transformation

Here's the final truth: **You already have everything you need inside you to succeed.** God has equipped you with a mind to think, a heart to feel, a body to act, and a spirit connected to His.

The Renew4D 90-Day Journal isn't a magic solution. It's simply a tool that helps you steward what God has already given you.

Your future self is waiting.
The Seven Mountains need your influence.
The world needs who you're becoming.

It's time to stop dreaming and start doing.

"Anything above zero compounds."

Now go get that journal and begin your transformation.

✿ Renew4D Reflection: Write It Down, Change Your Life

Discover the lie you've believed.

You believed that remembering was enough. Reflecting on goals, dreams, or habits was just as effective as taking action on them. That your intentions mattered more than your systems, but the truth is: if you don't write it, you won't run with it. Without a vision written down, purpose fades and momentum dies.

Develop truth statements rooted in God's Word.

- "Write the vision and make it plain… that he may run who reads it." – Habakkuk 2:2
- "Where there is no vision, the people perish." – Proverbs 29:18
- "Faith without works is dead." – James 2:17
- "You are a temple of the Holy Spirit… honor God with your body." – 1 Corinthians 6:19–20

Write these truths. Speak them daily. Journal them until your life starts to reflect them.

Deploy daily habits that strengthen mental and spiritual resilience.

Start journaling every morning, afternoon, and night. Don't overthink it. Just write. Begin with your goals, habits, thoughts, prayers, and progress. Use SMART goals for clarity:

- Specific: What exactly are you trying to do?
- Measurable: How will you know if you're on track?
- Achievable: Is it realistic and within your capacity?
- Relevant: Does it align with your calling and values?
- Time-bound: When will you achieve it?

Track your body, soul, mind, and spirit daily. Use the Four D's to reflect:

- Discover what God revealed today.
- Develop new habits or insights.
- Deploy your actions, obedience, or risk taken.
- Duplicate by sharing your journey with others.

Pro Tip: Schedule time at 5 AM (or your preferred hour) to journal, exercise, learn, and pray. Anchor your mornings and evenings with reflection and gratitude.

Duplicate this mindset shift in others by modeling and mentoring.

Teach your family, small group, or team how to journal with purpose. Gift them a Renew4D Journal. Show them what consistent reflection looks like. Invite accountability into your vision. Post one truth you are journaling weekly. Mentor someone new through the practice. Remind them that anything above zero compounds, and journaling turns invisible progress into visible victory.

CELEBRATION TIME

You just unlocked the secret that separates the 5% who achieve their dreams from the 95% who don't! You've discovered that writing down your goals, habits, and dreams isn't just helpful—it's the difference between wishful thinking and actual transformation. You now have the SMART goals framework, understand how the 4 D's apply to Spirit, Mind, Soul, and Body, and know that journaling turns invisible progress into visible victory. Most importantly, you've learned that "if you don't write it, you won't run with it."

Put this book down and grab a journal right now. Write down your first SMART goal using the format you just learned. Tell someone about your commitment to daily journaling and invite them into your accountability journey. Set your 5 AM alarm (or whatever time works) to start your Victory Hour tomorrow. You've just joined the elite 5% who actually write down their vision—and that deserves immediate celebration.

Don't put off being happy for the sake of growing and grinding.

17. Closing: From Renew4D to Released

Now I'm commissioning you. I'm sending you henceforth into the battlefield, onto your mountain of influence, into the world to be an agent of change. An agent of Renewal. Go make disciples. Go make disciples who make disciples. Go live out your dream. Go make millions. Go give millions. Go help others. Go guide others. Go take back those mountains. Go be a light in the world. Be salt. Give your sphere of influence a little seasoning. Be a thermostat, not a thermometer. Be blessed!

The Blessing

The Lord bless you
and keep you;
The Lord make his face shine on you
and be gracious to you;
The Lord turn his face toward you
and give you peace.

-   Numbers 6:24-26

Now, go into all the world, share your journey, and make disciples. Go and be blessed!

Resources

Throughout my journey, these books, podcasts, apps, and tools played a huge role in shaping my growth. They're not just recommendations. They're resources I personally used and still lean on. I hope they inspire and equip you on your own path to renewal.

Books

- *The Power to Change* by Craig Groeschel
- *The Common Rule* by Justin Whitmel Earley
- *Practicing the Way* by John Mark Comer
- *Atomic Habits* by James Clear
- *The 5 AM Club* by Robin Sharma
- *Winning the War in Your Mind* by Craig Groeschel
- *Resilience* by John Eldredge
- *Genius Foods* by Max Lugavere
- *Find Your Why* by Simon Sinek
- *Crush It!* by Gary V
- *Level Up* by Rob Dial
- *Think and Grow Rich* by Napoleon Hill
- *Rise and Grind* by Damond John
- *X: Multiply Your God-Given Potential* by John Bevere

Podcasts / Influencers

- **Rob Dial** – Mindset/Personal Development
- **Ed Mylett** – Motivation/Leadership
- **Mel Robbins** – Mindset
- **Simon Sinek** – Leadership
- **John Eldredge** – Masculinity / Soul Health
- **Dan Martell** – Productivity / Business Growth
- **Robin Sharma** – Personal Mastery / Leadership

- **Lewis Howes** – The School of Greatness / Performance
- **Gary Vaynerchuk (Gary V)** – Entrepreneurship / Branding
- **Brendon Burchard** – High Performance Habits / Coaching
- **Russell Brunson** – Business/Marketing
- **Dave Ramsey** – Finance
- **Tara-Leigh Cobble** – The Bible Recap
- **John Bevere** – Discipleship
- **Mark Hyman** – Health/Nutrition
- **Andrew Huberman** – Neuroscience
- **Max Lugavere** – Health & Nutrition

Apps

- **Pause App** by John Eldredge – for prayer, mental reset
- **SuppCo App** – supplement tracker and validator
- **Yuka** – food scanner for nutrition/ingredients
- **MyFitnessPal** – calorie & diet tracking
- **Atoms.** by James Clear – habit tracker
- **Fitbit (Garmin, Apple Health)** – Activity, sleep, heart rate monitoring, exercise, step counter
- **Goodreads** – Track your reading goals
- **Apple Podcasts (or any podcast app)** – Stream many of the podcasts referenced in this book

Music

- **Spotify - Renew4D Worship Playlist**
  - Listen Here: bit.ly/Renew4DSpotify

My Supplement Stack

Brain / Cognition

- **Lion's Mane Extract** – Supports brain function, focus, and

memory.
- **NMNH (Nicotinamide Mononucleotide)** – Cellular energy & anti-aging (NAD+ support).
- **L-Theanine** – Calms the mind without drowsiness; great paired with caffeine.

Fitness / Recovery

- **Creatine Monohydrate** – Boosts strength, muscle energy, and performance.
- **Collagen Peptides** – Joint, skin, and connective tissue support.
- **Organic Vegan Protein (Orgain)** – Protein + fiber for muscle repair and weight management.
- **Essential Amino Acids** – Muscle recovery and lean mass support.

Heart & Cholesterol

- **CoQ10** – Cellular energy and heart health.
- **Red Yeast Rice** – Naturally supports healthy cholesterol.
- **Ultra Omega-3** – Supports cardiovascular and brain function.

Liver Detox & Organ Support

- **NAC (N-Acetyl Cysteine)** – Detox + glutathione support (antioxidant).
- **Dandelion Root** – Natural liver and digestive cleanser.
- **Milk Thistle** – Classic herb for liver regeneration and detox.
- **Turmeric Curcumin** – Anti-inflammatory + liver/bone support.

⚖️ Metabolic & Weight Support

- **Citrus Bergamot** – Cholesterol and metabolic regulation.
- **Chromium Picolinate** – Blood sugar balance and appetite control.
- **Berberine** – Natural support for insulin sensitivity and blood sugar regulation.

🧘 Stress & Hormonal Health

- **Ashwagandha** – Adaptogen for stress, mood, and energy.
- **Vitamin D3 + K2** – Bone strength, immune, and hormone support.

🧂 Minerals & Longevity

- **Magnesium Glycinate** – Muscle, nerve, sleep, and joint health.
- **Mineral Sea Salt (like Baja or Celtic)** – Electrolytes and trace minerals.
- **Resveratrol** – Anti-aging and heart health

🌱 Multinutrient / All-in-One

- **AG1 Next Gen** – A daily foundational blend with vitamins, adaptogens, probiotics, and more.

About the Author

Jessee Lovaas is a leadership coach, mentor, and author with over two decades of hands-on experience developing people from the inside out. For more than 20 years, Jessee has led in the trenches, training teams, counseling individuals, mentoring leaders, and instilling a deep sense of purpose, discipline, and identity across a wide spectrum of ages and backgrounds.

From high-capacity professionals to teens navigating their formative years, Jessee has helped thousands discover who they are, develop sustainable habits, deploy their God-given gifts, and duplicate that impact in the lives of others. His work spans leadership development, organizational coaching, personal renewal, and ministry support—always rooted in the belief that true transformation happens when your body, soul, mind, and spirit are aligned under God's design.

Drawing from years of experience in education, ministry, business leadership, and character development, Jessee created the Renew4D framework—a practical, biblically grounded system designed to guide people through personal renewal and growth. At the heart of his message is a passion for helping others unlock their potential, embrace their identity in Christ, and live with intentionality in every area of life.

Jessee's work combines proven coaching methods, timeless wisdom, and spiritual truth to help individuals not only grow—but multiply their impact. Whether through books, workshops, coaching, or speaking, he brings a unique ability to connect, challenge, and inspire lasting change.

Jessee is the husband of a fantastic wife, Rebekah. He's a father of two beautiful kiddos, Henry and Savannah. And, he's a pet dad to Copper, the 14-year-old family Puggle.

www.Renew4D.com
Follow me @Renew4D
Instagram / Facebook / TikTok / Youtube / X / LinkedIn